ALL HIS GRACE

DONALD SOPER

LONDON : THE EPWORTH PRESS

THE EPWORTH PRESS
(FRANK H. CUMBERS)
25-35 City Road, London, E.C.1

MELBOURNE CAPE TOWN
NEW YORK TORONTO

SET IN MONOTYPE IMPRINT AND PRINTED IN
GREAT BRITAIN BY THE CAMELOT PRESS LTD
LONDON AND SOUTHAMPTON

Contents

Introduction

SO many books have been written about Jesus and His Cross, and written by such wise and saintly Christians, that an addition to their number should be made only with a clearly defined and sufficient reason. Yet I will not follow the fashion of apologizing for attempting to write yet one more book on this eternal theme. I lay claim to no deep insight which can perceive and set down truths about the Passion of our Lord which have hitherto remained hidden. I possess no outstanding qualities of goodness which bring me closer than my fellows to my Saviour, and therefore enhance my understanding of His atoning love. Nor have I read the Passion literature and the history of the early Church so widely that I can bring together the sifted wisdom of wide research and present a composite picture containing the worthiest elements of Christian thinking on the Cross. From time to time I have axes to grind, but I should regard it as gravely improper to use the occasion of Lent and a book like this for such purposes.

I presume to find a sufficient reason in another realm altogether—not in the special qualifications of the writer, but in the fact that he has a unique personality, however commonplace his attainments may be. Such a claim would be presumptuous only in one who entirely disregarded or denied one of the greatest truths that the Christian faith utters about men. We are encouraged by our Lord to believe that every one of us is a child of God, and that each is of infinite worth because all are of infinite variety. The same light of love that shines upon us all is differently refracted by each because none of us is quite like any other. Quite apart from the differences that we develop, there remain the differences which are our birth-marks. Herein lies one of the great glories of this amazing human life with which God has endowed us.

If I take God's gifts of truth and love and make them my

own, I am doing something that has never been done before in quite the same way, because there has never been anyone quite like me. Better still, if I show forth these truths and that love in my own life and in my own words, I am adding something which is unprecedented and unique to the store of human knowledge and understanding. The required qualifications are not special gifts, but personal honesty and simplicity. If, without affectation or pretence, I can be myself, then the Cross of Jesus can be reflected in my life and transmitted by my words with new emphasis and stresses, which may by His grace redound to His glory and the blessing of others. What therefore I cannot do out of my own attainments, God can do through me, just as I am, provided that I allow no smear of insincerity to stain His image.

It is in this strong belief that I am encouraged to write what follows this introduction. Moreover, this same belief prescribes the substance of the only kind of book which I ought to undertake. I shall strive after no novelty and attempt no startling revaluation of the meaning of Calvary. What I shall try to do is to consider some qualities which our Lord displays in His Passion, as they have impressed themselves upon my mind and heart. I hope then to turn to the practical question as to the way or ways in which these qualities may be imparted to the life of the believer. It will not, I think, be gainsaid that there is much glib talking from pulpits and in pews about this all-important issue. 'Come to Jesus' is the sneer of the heckler who pretends to think that all preaching is a racket. 'Come to Jesus' is also the rather vapid and escapist phrase we are tempted to use rather than face the very real problem of how the goodness of Jesus can possibly affect the lives of people living in the twentieth century. His goodness is a magnificent example, but is it no more than that? The last part of this short book will be concerned with this problem, and will offer the beginnings of an answer to it.

In neither part of the book shall I be especially interested in theories of the Atonement. Necessary as those theories are to the economy of the Church, they are liable to become agents of division and diversion. They divide because they tend to concentrate the efficacy of our Lord's redeeming work on that part of it which can be expressed in precise words, and consequently upon the various and separable forms in which those words can be arranged; yet every pilgrim of Calvary knows that there is infinitely more than intellectual truth in the Cross. They divert because Jesus Himself is the object of our faith, and our supreme business is with Him as personal Saviour, rather than with ideas about Him or even the most sacred truths that He proclaims from the Cross.

Furthermore, the overall tendency among those who concentrate their attention upon the doctrines of our Lord's Atonement is often to produce a state of mind which looks no farther than these doctrines and therefore makes no sufficient effort to understand the moral and spiritual temper of our Lord Himself who atones. In fact, it would appear to me that our knowledge of, or acquaintance with, the metaphysical and theological attributes of our Lord has outrun our appreciation of His character. I remember Martin Luther's insistence on the primacy of that 'moral union' that Jesus enjoyed with the Father, and I should not be discontented if what I shall try to say is regarded principally as having to do with the moral approach to the Cross of Jesus. In the simplest of words, I want to know more, and I want others to know more, of the sublime virtues of Jesus Christ. 'There was no other good enough to pay the price of sin' says for me something which strikes more quickly and deeply to my heart than do most of the great ecclesiastical statements about the Cross. It is the goodness of my Lord which challenges my sinfulness. It is His goodness which acts decisively on the broad stage of human history. It is that goodness which alters everything and makes all things new. It is that goodness which takes away my sin and the sin of others and opens the Kingdom of Heaven to all believers. So to face that goodness, to open my life to its warmth and strength, to see it confronted by the sin of the world, and from the bitter struggle with that sin to see it issue triumphant in the Resurrection and the Redeemed Society, is the all-absorbing vocation of the penitent sinner, and the equally all-important calling of the justified believer.

I would wish the reader, therefore, to consider the moral excellence of Jesus against the background of the Cross whereon He suffered and from which the various aspects of that infinite goodness are seen in typical and critical splendour.

There will be, of course, no attempt to present a comprehensive picture of the moral character of Jesus Christ, and any reader hoping for some analytical or physiological treatment of our Lord's personality must remain unsatisfied. Instead, I shall endeavour to relate some of the great moral categories like 'single-mindedness', 'courage', 'meekness', and others, to the Jesus who particularly reveals His nature to us in the Passion. I shall try to say something of the way in which those categories look from the foot of the Cross. Because moral attributes do not fit into watertight compartments of the personality, it will be impossible clearly to separate these attributes from one another. I hope that the impression will grow with the reader, that the qualities of our Lord 'build each other up in love' and help to yield the picture of the one man who in this earthly life has been completely integrated—the one 'full man' who has ever lived.

I would then wish the reader to consider whether what he has found is in fact a Gospel, the announcement of good news for him and for everybody else. I have just used words big with meaning and tremendous in what they imply. Can it happen like this? I would say no more here than that I believe in the Gospel because the Jesus who sets me the example of the good life is the same Jesus who has come to me and offered to live in me so that I may live that good life. That is the power of God unto salvation.

For writer and reader alike, I append some advice given by G. K. Chesterton to those who would 'save their souls alive'. You should think, said he, of your soul as a window; and there are two things to be done with a window—the first is to clean it and the second is to forget it. May we, who look at Jesus dying on the Cross, first be made clean by His amazing love, and then become so lost to ourselves that others may see Him clearly in us.

D.S.

ONE

Single-mindedness

AS far back as I can remember, the single-mindedness of Jesus Christ has confronted me with a persistent challenge, maybe because my own experience has been so much that of double or even multiple-mindedness. I can sing with an all-too-keen appreciation of its truth:

> *Though what I dream and what I do*
> *In my weak days are always two,*
> *Help me, oppressed by things undone,*
> *O Thou, whose deeds and dreams were one!*

This neat and almost mathematical diagnosis speaks to my condition, except that it oversimplifies that condition. The trouble is, that so often my motives seem to be much more complicated still. I could almost wish that double-mindedness were the extent of my complaint; but I have been conscious so often of many voices calling from many directions, and have been plagued by the sense that I am never sure that I can respond wholeheartedly to any one of them. It is this lack of unity or integration in me that serves as a dark background to the vivid, blazing simplicity of Jesus Christ. One thing I have learnt, and that is how unprofitable it is to attempt some rational explanation of this many-creatured jungle inside me. Though I begin with the effort to be rational, I soon slip over into rationalization, and the last stage is often more perplexing than the first. How much better it is to look away from myself to what, I am persuaded, is the pattern of true unity—to the Master who was self-determined by one persistent and consuming purpose.

The Gospels speak with an unmistakable voice of this one increasing purpose. Jesus, the dark-skinned youth of twelve years, was irresistibly drawn to the Temple and to its Doctors.

His astonishment at His parents' concern about Him was a perfectly natural token of His single-mindedness. There was nothing in it of unfilial indifference. 'Wist ye not that I must be in my Father's House?' was the unaffected and simple testimony to the wholeheartedness of His boyish convictions. This wholeheartedness of the adolescent Jesus was obviously much more deeply rooted than the decision of a youth of comparable age today (say sixteen or seventeen) to be a farmer, or a lawyer, or a racing-driver, or a teacher. It was the response to a sense of divine obligation and not the desire for self-expression. Herein surely lay the key to the subsequent pattern of Jesus Christ's earthly ministry.

This integrating power was transcendent rather than immanent. It was the categorically imperative 'I must be about my Father's business' that created and maintained His single-mindedness. We possess (as yet) no positive evidence of the life of our Lord between the Temple episode and His baptism by John, but there is eloquent negative testimony from that period that His powers and energies were directed to what He knew to be this divine vocation.

One of the critical matters is that of marriage. We know that Jesus did not marry a wife, and there are only two possible reasons to account for this extraordinary fact. One is that physically and temperamentally he was 'not the marrying kind'. This canard has been dressed up in ecclesiastical jargon and proclaimed even as a dogma by occasional theologians of the Christian Church, in their anxiety to enhance the spirituality of our Lord. I will not delay to demolish such inventions, except to point out that everything in the Gospel indicates the psychological normalcy of Jesus. He spoke of earthly, and particularly of sexual passions, with the authority of a master who had faced them and tamed them.

The only other sufficient reason is that His Father's business was so urgent that He had deliberately to set aside the joys and intimacies of a family life in order to fulfil God's destiny in Him. It may be that He joined Himself to a Jewish religious order which prescribed celibacy. Such a speculation is, however, irrelevant to our present purpose. The important thing is that it was in this dominant mood of dedication that He came to the Jordan. His baptism there ratified His sense of call. By the humble observance of this Jewish rite He made public His avowed intention to do His Father's will to the exclusion of every competing claim.

This single and unswerving intention underscored every episode in the public ministry of our Lord, but it is on the Cross that His absolute dedication of purpose to His mission becomes for me overwhelming. From the moment that He set His face steadfastly toward Jerusalem, the more easy and familiar relationship between Jesus and His disciples was replaced by a growing sense on their part of the profound gulf which separated them from their Master. They had already marvelled at His moral purity, and with growing appreciation recognized the iron discipline with which He faced all sorts of temptation. Now this admiration grew so much deeper as they were confronted with His sense of committal (surely the exact word in this context). I imagine that this must have marked the turning point in their realization of His Divine Person. Up to this time they had felt obliged to stand in His presence out of respect for His pre-eminent qualities; now they felt compelled to kneel in awe before His consuming purpose. This awful concentration of Jesus becomes more and more vivid the nearer they and we come to Calvary.

I remember a cynic on Tower Hill complaining of what he called the 'morbid preoccupation of Jesus with dying'. I do not think that the phrase was his own, but the thought behind it is quite widespread, particularly among young people today. They resent the idea of this young man, who had so much to give to the world, fixing his intention upon a cross which would take Him out of it. Once upon a time I shared something of their attitude, and it is not merely because I am older that I have now changed. Watching Jesus going to His death has taught me the marvellous economy of our Lord's character. He had no preoccupation with either living or dying. His whole mind was set to fulfil His vocation. How resolutely He put away the challenging alternatives to the Jerusalem journey, and this not at all because He intended to die, but because He was completely set upon the one thing needful—to manifest the Father's love. He was consumed with the desire to show on earth the Father's Kingdom face to face with the spiritual forces of His day, and to show it, moreover, in the capital city of His people.

This absolute clarity of purpose gave to our Lord an equally clear perception of the course of events that would inexorably follow His entry into the city. He knew that He must die, because He knew that there could be no compromise on His part and there would be no change of heart among His enemies. His great prayer in the Garden was for strength, not for guidance. His appeal to His disciples to stand with Him was not made in the hope that by their doing so the Cross might be avoided, but rather with the intention that its effects might be enhanced and quickened. His demeanour before His accusers was controlled by the same over-arching unity of purpose. He was not prepared to defend Himself, and most of the time before the High Priests and before Herod and Pilate He kept silence. When He spoke, it was to witness to His allegiance to the Father and to emphasize His obedience to His Father's will. Nothing else was relevant.

So the story moves on to the last dreadful act on Calvary; and here again it is mainly one of silence. 'Seven words He spoke, seven words of love, and all three hours His silence cried.' It cried not only 'for mercy on the souls of men', but for recognition that there was little need for words. There was no need at all for eleventh hour exhortations to those disciples who were brave enough to stand beneath His Cross, no need for dying instructions about what they should do, no anxiety for the morrow. 'Sufficient unto the day was the evil thereof.' After He had comforted His mother, and seen to it that His torturers were offered forgiveness and His penitent fellow victim was offered Paradise, He said: 'It is finished.' The one single thing He had begun to do thirty and more years ago in Nazareth He had accomplished within the limits of a human life. In serenity He died.

As Christians have looked upon Jesus dying, they have

always felt, with sure perception, that here is an altar at which to worship, rather than a pulpit from which to preach. Yet because the merit of Christ's death must be announced, we cannot but pass on to others what we have ourselves found at the foot of that altar.

To me there are certain strands in the pattern of single-mindedness to be seen in Jesus Christ that are especially impressive. Standing afar off as I do, I have yet come nearer to Him as I have the more fully appreciated particular characteristics of that sublime unity of His heart and will and mind.

His single-mindedness was articulate. Even as a boy, Jesus brought to the conscious level of clear speech the sense of vocation which was growing within him. With His disciples He was at pains to declare this one 'increasing purpose'. He set it in the context of a servant. We may find it well nigh impossible in this twentieth century to think ourselves into the attitude of a Galilean Jew in the first century toward the word 'servant'. Whatever genuine effort we make must lead us toward the idea of a man whose very personality was vested, so to say, in that of His master. The servant lived his whole life, or was compelled so to do, obeying the will of the master who practically owned him. Jesus must have repeated again and again to His disciples that He was both the servant of God and their servant for God's sake. On that matter He left them in no possible doubt, and at the superbly dramatic and moving episode of the feet-washing He imprinted this idea ineradicably on their memories. I find it impossible to escape the conviction that Jesus moved to His death with an eagerness so to use all the public and horrible trappings of a crucifixion as to make public, for all to see, the purpose He had come to fulfil. Moreover, it seems to me beyond doubt that His public witness to His vocation was not only a comfort to those who received that witness, but also a profound source of strength to Himself. The power that sustained our Lord was a fire that burned within Him. Yet surely that fire was constantly replenished by the fact that the disciples had warmed their hands at its blaze. 'For their sakes I sanctify myself' are words that live with me as I think of the single-mindedness of Jesus. The making known to others of a conviction or an intention is always a bulwark of strength in the day of temptation. If I hold a purpose secret, then in temptation my resolution is weakened by the reflection that no one will be the wiser if I succumb. If Jesus felt it necessary to strengthen His own will by inviting His disciples into the open secret of His vocation, how much more do I need that added power which such a shared vocation provides. Let me make haste to nail my colours to the mast for all to see. They may then survive the fiercest storm.

Again, the single-mindedness of Jesus was a deep source of His serenity. Jesus is the one fully integrated man who has lived upon this earth. I suppose most of us would give a vague assent to these two statements without inquiring with any care into the actual relationship between personal integration and personal serenity. Jesus was at peace with Himself; that is the meaning of serenity. And peace of any kind is a positive condition; it is not just the absence of strife, any more than harmony is the absence of discord. Peace is the harmonious relationship of the various notes in the spiritual scale, in the same way that music is the harmonious relationship of the notes of a keyboard.

Jesus testifies in His every action, and typically in His dying, that the dominant purpose of doing God's will is in fact the open secret of that personal harmony which is serenity. It is an affective purpose which possesses the power to expel doubt, perplexity, and anxiety as nothing else can. Of course, in the case of a sinner like me, to know what is God's will is often most perplexing, but an honest review of my own life reveals that in many particulars I have always known deep down what I ought to do. It has been my own refusal to centre my actions upon the known will of God which has bedevilled my mind and plagued me so often with anxieties and fears. Today, with the vast increase in awareness of intellectual problems, an awareness of which our fathers were largely ignorant, this unrest is vastly complicated.

One of the most frequent results is a kind of moral paralysis.

I can think of many who frequent Hyde Park on Sundays who appear to be a sort of repository for innumerable ideas and competing moral claims. No final solution is ever reached, no practical step is ever taken. They are inveterate arguers, and sometimes sympathetic listeners, but their lives are an unceasing conference, as it were, wherein they possess no power to take a vote or accept a proposition. For many of their doubts I have a fellow feeling; in fact I share some of them. Of one thing I have no doubt at all. They are restless and frustrated, and are complete strangers to that peace of mind which passes, but never by-passes, understanding. If they could arrange their doubts around some central point of activity or purpose, those doubts would appear in a totally different and more genial light. That is exactly what Jesus did.

There is nothing irreverent in saying that our Lord's knowledge was incomplete, or that His mind ranged over many problems to which He found no final answer. The Gospels take care to remind us of the nescience of Jesus. 'Of that day and hour knoweth no man, not even the Son.' The Jesus who marvelled, was puzzled even, at unbelief, and who said 'How is it?' to disciples in whose lack of faith He was disappointed, might have been halted between two opinions time and again had He not been driven forward by a dominant impulse which overrode them. His single-mindedness enabled Him to carry these doubts with Him as He went steadfastly forward to do His Father's will. Having chosen the better part, our Lord found the one thing needful—the serenity of living close to God. He offers that same serenity to us, and on the same terms.

I will write of one other element in that single-mindedness of Jesus, which has burnt itself into my experience, and I will venture to use a most prosaic word to identify it. The single-mindedness of Jesus was detailed. Let me call to mind the explicit words of our Lord, which we especially remember on Passion Sunday. 'And they were in the way going up to Jerusalem; and Jesus went before them: and they were amazed; and as they followed, they were afraid. And he took

B

again the twelve, and began to tell them what things should happen unto him, saying, Behold, we go up to Jerusalem; and the Son of man shall be delivered unto the chief priests, and unto the scribes; and they shall condemn him to death, and shall deliver him to the Gentiles: and they shall mock him, and shall scourge him, and shall spit upon him, and shall kill him: and the third day he shall rise again.' Luke sees these words principally against the backcloth of prophecy, but surely they bear eloquent witness to the precision with which Jesus looked to the fulfilment of His mission. Commentators may be right to regard the detailed declarations of our Lord as the exact acceptance on His part of Old Testament prophecy. Surely it is of equal importance to see in them a plan of campaign in which each eventuality was considered and each detail anticipated. Jesus was not the passive instrument of prophecy. He was the supreme strategist who grasped the broad outline of God's plan for Him. He was the supreme tactician who worked out that plan in detail. In these, as in so many other matters, our Lord was the master of insight rather than foresight.

Jesus would have little sympathy for the vague generalities in which Christianity is so often decked out in the modern world. The Church has often elevated ignorance about the future to the status of a virtue, as if it were impious to know too much about tomorrow; but the Sermon on the Mount is always perverted when it is made to support indifference about tomorrow rather than to condemn anxiety about it. The truth is that no Christian can copy the single-mindedness of his Saviour without copying also the care with which Jesus worked at, and worked out, God's purpose. It is impossible to seek the Kingdom of God with heart and soul and strength unless that Kingdom has boundaries which can be prescribed and a constitution which can be planned. Similarly, it is impossible to advance toward that Kingdom until the terrain that lies between us and it has been mapped. Single-mindedness peters out in escapism unless it is thought of as both a pilgrimage and a campaign. I do not possess the marvellous insight that enabled Jesus to make unerring judgements about the future and to anticipate every move of the enemy. Nevertheless, I am not thereby absolved from the duty of working out, as best I can, the dictated implications of my call. I would append a word of testimony here.

Although the political, economic, and social attitudes that I have adopted in order to express my own loyalty to Jesus Christ have often, no doubt, been faltering and always imperfect, yet they are the salt of single-mindedness, without which it cannot be preserved. That I have proved. This working out of our salvation with appropriate fear and trembling is marvellously proclaimed from the Cross. Jesus declares in His death the nature and the limits of our task under God. He demands of us that we press on with our discipleship to the limits of human understanding and effort before we dare to claim that 'All things work together for good to them that love God'.

I want to be able to say: 'This one thing I do—forgetting the things that are behind, I press on.'

Again, the single-mindedness of Jesus was comprehensive. In this matter of comprehensiveness, I would suggest, there lies the essential difference between the *dévot* and the 'fanatic', between the Quaker with a 'concern in his heart' and the crank with a 'bee in his bonnet'. It is quite impossible for a man to centre his life upon an objective or a goal which, by its very restricted nature, can fulfil only certain limited capacities that lie within him. The sportsman who lives for his games, the stamp collector for his stamps, the gardener for his flowers, are instances of single-mindedness that is good so far as it goes, but is quite inadequate in size to be worthy of a life's work. When these objectives are given exclusive place in the affections, they invariably reduce their exponents to unbalance and maladjustment. Single-minded attachment to unworthy, as well as to inadequate, objectives, as in the case of the miser and the gourmand, leads even more obviously to perversion. Any fair-minded inquirer who comes to the New Testament records about Jesus must be impressed by the almost total absence of any suggestion of fanaticism. One accusation that nobody succeeded in substantiating, even in the eyes of his most vicious enemies, was that Jesus was a deluded crank. He made even those fiercest enemies take Him seriously. He compelled even the contemptuous Romans to see the moral size of His message and the world-sweep of His Gospel. It is as if He says to friend and foe alike: 'If a man is going to set his heart on one thing, let him take good care to see that that one thing is big enough to enlist his every gift and capacity, for only then can it produce an integrated life.' This, in clumsy words, is what Jesus did say with limpid clarity in those oft-repeated words: 'Seek ye first the Kingdom of God and its righteousness, and all these things shall be added unto you.' In fact the Sermon on the Mount is a series of variations upon the theme that blessedness is the by-product of a God-centred life, and the cult of God's Kingdom is the promise of perfection.

I cannot escape the conviction that Christians so often degenerate into frowning cranks, not because their conversion experience—i.e. their integration—is forsaken, but because it becomes attached to ends which are too small to rescue it from fanaticism. I think of those who down the years have assailed the Press with correspondence about Sabbatarianism, who have badgered their fellows about the 'satanic weed' or the 'devil's brew', who have clamoured for the barring of dancing and even the proscription of the theatre. Now, I am a tee-totaller and I intend to remain one. What is more, I know the difference between Cydrax and Cyder, and I do not feel compelled for reasons of health to drink wine on the Continent because the water is not to be trusted. Furthermore, I take a most serious view of the desecration and commercialization of Sunday, and know how pleasure-mad many people of all ages are today. The trouble is, that when Christians become absorbed in, and identified with, those important, but second-ary, issues, they lose their spiritual balance. The attempt to express all their mind and zeal through such inadequate media leads to a form of religious mania—the balance of their spiritual life is disturbed.

The somewhat pawky valedictory advice which Dr Oman is reported to have given to the theological students who had finished their course and were about to enter upon the work of the ministry—'Take large texts, gentlemen, and when they persecute you in one city flee into the next'—is profound as well as funny. Let me believe sufficiently in the moral stature of my own soul to be sure that I must not squander my life on a triviality or dedicate it to any cause which can exercise only some aspects of it. Let me copy my Lord who found unity and serenity in giving Himself up to God's service and offering Himself for God's Kingdom. In such service, and for such a Kingdom, He was able to bring under control every thought and every feeling and all His will. So it must be with me.

TWO

Courage

COURAGE is one of the apparently simple virtues, and most of us would think that we know what it is even if we do not practise it. Yet, as anyone who has made the attempt to define courage realizes, this appearance of simplicity is quite deceptive. I suppose it is induced by the fact that the opposite of courage is easily detected and simple to recognize. Cowardice, as the absence of a certain quality which we intuitively recognize as admirable, is self-evident. Men can be deceived here, as everywhere, and ascribe cowardice to actions and attitudes which turn out to be anything but cowardly, but generally cowardice is the obvious failure to meet certain difficult or dangerous operations with an appropriate response. A coward is one who fails to display a positive virtue in the face of danger or threat, and that failure is much more clearly seen than the actual virtue which it suggests but does not define. In fact, the more I think of courage the more complex does the problem of defining it appear. What do words like 'physical courage' mean when they are intended to distinguish one particular aspect of this virtue from another—mental courage, for example. I can easily see the difference between the absence of fear and the problem of fear, and my experience tells me that 'hot' actions belong to a very different order from 'cold' actions; but what is the intrinsic nature of courage? And is there such a virtue as Christian courage, as distinct, say, from Muslim courage?

The narrative of the life of Jesus in the Gospels, and particularly the narrative of His death, is a storehouse of information about courage. I have heard many criticisms of the impracticability of our Lord's teaching and a few criticisms of His character. Dr Montefiore, for instance, in his book on the teaching of Jesus, complains of the lack of charity in Jesus for the Pharisees (a criticism which I feel is singularly lacking in judgement, in that it confuses the scathing things that Jesus said about the Pharisees with the love in which He died for them as much as for any sinners). But I cannot remember anyone, even the most hostile of critics, calling Jesus a coward. Even those who would regard His morality as a 'slave morality' would yet think of Jesus as the noblest and bravest of slaves.

As I think of the ministry of Jesus, and especially of the events crowded into its last few days, courage appears as an element in everything He did. To use an illustration from the chemistry book: courage was the 'base' of His actions and His demeanour. He set His face toward Jerusalem, knowing all too well what awaited Him there, and knowing just as well that He would have to walk the last miles of that 'Via Dolorosa' alone and deserted; He was a young man of infinite zest as well as of infinite goodness, and He was deliberately choosing pain and imprisonment and horrible death when life offered its treasures to Him with both hands.

I am told that Isaac Watts in his superb hymn, 'When I survey the wondrous Cross', originally wrote, as the second line, not 'On which the Prince of Glory died', but 'Where the young Prince of Glory died'. It is true that the stress of the more familiar version is better suited to a tune like *Rockingham*, yet to sing 'Where the young Prince of Glory died' is for me a sudden and penetrating experience of the sublime courage of this young man who for our sakes 'endured the Cross, despising the shame'. The very objectiveness of the Passion narrative tends to divert the attention of the reader from the courage which irradiates each successive stage of it. Modern biographers confronted with this epic story would almost certainly have paused time and again to emphasize the self-control of our Lord in these most exacting and fearsome circumstances. We are not told that He 'squared His shoulders' to meet those who had come to arrest Him, or that He held His head high when the soldiers tortured Him, or that He 'bit His lip' when they drove in the nails. For me the record is infinitely more moving because of the absence of these aids to our imagination, but let me not forget the impact of these horrible events on my Lord's body and mind and heart. What courage there was in His long silence in the Judgement Hall! How brave He was in the face of weariness, prolonged interrogation and scourging! How splendidly He mastered the natural feelings of desolation, the prospects of dying in the fly-blown heat, the knowledge that no one could fully understand what He was doing, and that most would pass by in indifference and in scorn!

Coming as a pilgrim to the Cross, the Christian must be very careful lest he impudently imagines that he knows how Jesus felt as 'He hung and suffered there'. The suffering of a perfect man must not only be different in degree from the suffering of a sinner like me; it must also be different in kind. Like the penitent thief, to some extent, we merit the 'just reward of our sins, but this man hath done nothing amiss'. The awareness of perfect innocence on the part of Jesus must have brought with it an exquisite kind of pain, of which we can know almost nothing. It demanded a demonstration of courage before which we can only bow in wonder.

Of the demeanour of our Lord on the Cross the record is economical to a degree. I have taken part for many years in Good Friday Three-Hours Services and have spoken from time to time on the Seven Words from the Cross. I have proved what a deeply rewarding experience this vigil can be and have also found how these sacred words of our Lord build themselves up into a unity of meaning. Particularly they reveal to me the quiet heroism of a man ruling His spirit with unbroken discipline—a discipline which is the more vividly seen to be heroic as imagination plays on the horrible pain and misery of such a way of dying.

I do not understand the significance of His words of desolation: 'My God, my God, why hast Thou forsaken me.' I confess to being dissatisfied with the explanation that Jesus was reciting a much beloved psalm—a psalm which begins in doubt and ends in confidence. I well remember as a boy rushing eagerly to Psalm 22 when this explanation was first offered to me. I remember even better the sense of disappointment as I read the psalm through. It did not seem to me then, and it does not seem to me now, that with all His knowledge of psalmody Jesus would have selected this one. However, it may well be that the fault is mine and that I am falling into the trap of claiming to know too exactly the mind of the Saviour. Suppose, however, that these words were uttered not in trust but in desolation. I will have nothing to do with the infamous suggestion, beloved of some totalitarian evangelists, that 'God turned His back on Jesus on the Cross', and that the cry was the realization that in fact God had forsaken Him. I venture another thought. The courageous spirit of Jesus drove His poor broken body to the limits of its endurance and tolerance. It was not His spirit that cracked into faithlessness; it was the body that temporarily took charge of that tortured spirit and brought the respite of delirium. What is more natural than this? It is the familiar experience of those whose suffering becomes unendurable.

We are eager to claim that Jesus was 'tempted in every point like as we are', and we dare not confine this assertion to the realm wherein we are tempted to do evil things or to think evil thoughts. The context is much wider. He was exposed to the same threats and challenges that we have to face, because He shared to the full the same human nature which is ours. We do well, in this twentieth century, especially in the light of the newer revelations of the mutual relationship of the body and the mind, to pay assiduous attention to this aspect of our Lord's earthly life. We must not, in the interests of His dominant spirit, underrate the 'dominion of the body'. Dr Inge once said that the trouble with Christianity is that we over-spiritualize it. Such a statement will sound scandalous to some, but it safeguards an inescapable truth. We have all our treasure in earthen vessels, and though those vessels do not determine their spiritual content, they invariably condition it. We must not try to exclude Jesus Christ from this general law. What more natural, then, than to accept the probability at least that at a certain stage in His agony that tortured body o'ercrowed for a while His spirit.

I find nothing unworthy or blasphemous in thinking that Jesus spoke those words of desolation in the delirium that unendurable pain had induced. On the contrary, they show in brighter relief the courage which nothing but the sheer force of His physical circumstance could affect. This cry does not represent a flaw in either our Lord's faith or His heroism. It serves to remind us of His humanity, and binds us to Him in the common bond of the same flesh, which was His and is ours.

In the brief record of the comment made by the Centurion, 'Surely this is a son of God', there is vouchsafed a glimpse of the impression which the courage of Jesus made upon those who watched Him die. We are instructed by the linguists to prefer the phrase 'a son of God' to the more familiar 'the Son of God', and common sense would suggest, quite apart from exegesis, that the Centurion would have been a most unlikely man to have used the second of these ascriptions. What impressed him so deeply in the man whose death he was supervising was His bravery, not His Messianic person. Like most Roman soldiers, he may have been curious about this new religious leader who so early was being 'liquidated', but he would have had no background of Jewish training and was probably confronting Jesus for the first time. He probably cared nothing for the claims and counter-claims of Messiah-ship. He may well have been contemptuous of the Jewish people and disgusted with their sectarian hatreds. Beginning his duties at Calvary as part of a brutal routine with which he was familiar, he was startled and arrested by the unique quality of this particular felon who was being done to death like the two others on either side of Him.

I dare say many miscreants died bravely on crosses in the days of our Lord. There has emerged an interesting comment on this theme in the recent arguments for and against capital punishment. It appears that generally in the face of death or torture more men are brave than are cowardly. That 'nothing becomes a man's life so much as his leaving of it', is much more than a sentimentality. Bravery was no new experience for a Centurion who had to watch men die on crosses. There is nothing fanciful, therefore, in saying that the courage of Jesus must have been so extraordinary as to suggest to this rough soldier that what distinguished His heroism from that of others was something supernatural. Perhaps the Centurion meant more than this; I cannot believe that he meant less. The courage of Jesus must have been a divine gift bestowed upon one who was, in a special sense, in touch with the supernatural Father to whom He prayed as He hung in the raging heat. Such was the strong feeling of the Centurion, and the words in which he said so come ringing down the centuries. We do not know what others felt or said, but those who waited to the end, watched the last dying moments, and heard the final confident cries of our Lord, may have attached all sorts of beliefs and superstitions to this dreadful event. What is unanimous is their sense of the awful courage of His dying. I find this unmistakable as I re-read the Passion narratives and try to breathe the psychological atmosphere that surrounds them.

We also know something of the impact of His courage on the disciples. There is little direct evidence, but there is an appreciable amount of reasonable inference, to suggest that the craven cowards whom He called His friends, who forsook Him and fled, leaving Him so terribly alone at His trial and scourging, had already picked up some fragments of His courage even while He was dying. John stood beneath the Cross with Mary, and this was dangerous for both of them. They were risking arrest from the Romans or assault from the Jews. A group of His friends apparently kept vigil through the terrible three hours, and they were ready to tend His body when the Romans were satisfied that there was no more life in it. The nucleus was a small band of women, who had more intrepidity than their menfolk, but I would hazard the guess that the amazing fortitude of Jesus had already begun to put some steel into the flabby spirits of the disciples. Jesus had said to Peter: 'I have prayed for you, and when you are converted strengthen your brethren.' I like to think of that conversion beginning after the cock had crowed, and to think of it leavening the life of Peter even while he watched His Master die. I am sure that the 'infection of a good courage' had much to do with it.

So it is that the simple and yet profound virtue of courage

is a common factor in the various episodes of the life of Jesus, especially in His passion, and is probably the most contagious of all the virtues demonstrated by our Lord. Its influence upon others seems to spring from the natural appreciation of courage which is the birthright even of the cowardly, as well as from the natural majesty with which it invests those who display it.

Let us consider, then, some of the insights into its deeper meaning which are given to us in our Lord's courage. These insights will be for edification, and should stimulate us to a new and effective use of this moral weapon wherewith we can 'fight the good fight' more effectively. The manifestation of Christian courage is one of the most powerful evangelical agents on which we can lay our hands.

I am sure that a most important clue to the meaning of courage for Jesus Christ is to be found in the comment which I have already made in describing the incidents of the last days of our Lord's earthly life. The bravery of Jesus was a quality that attached to, or was inherent in, His every action. To vary the metaphor—it was a kind of radiance that shone from everything He did. Courage in Jesus was one aspect of a noble life. We so often think of courage as an isolable virtue. Our failure to achieve it is probably for this very reason. We assume that courage can exist *in vacuo*, whereas it realizes itself only in the context of some other emotion or attitude. To put that much more simply: in the life of Jesus Christ there is no evidence that He deliberately sought to be brave, or in fact that He encouraged His disciples to be brave. Rather, He stressed the all-commanding will of God and the absolute authority which God ought to have in the life of man. Therefore, when we look for courage in Jesus, we shall find it when we find that Will of God clearly perceived and deeply felt.

It is possible to discover a relevant illustration of this truth in the realm of soldiering, a realm where obviously courage is a prime requirement. The standards of discipline and obedience in the crack regiments of the British Army are very high. The insistence on the instantaneous carrying out of given orders is taken on the parade-ground to limits which appear fatuous;

month after month the recruit practises the technique of recognizing a command and immediately making the appropriate response to it. Similarly, the 'spit and polish' that accompany these repeated manœuvres reach standards of precision and extravagance that to the outsider appear ridiculous. Now let there be no misunderstanding as far as I am concerned. I regard the whole business of soldiering as incompatible with the spirit of Jesus, and therefore sooner or later self-contradictory and farcical. But let us be fair to those who have worked out this curriculum of 'square-bashing' and 'spit and polish'. We must not underrate their intelligence. They know that the inculcation and stimulation of courage are best achieved, not by directly exhorting a soldier to be brave, but by drumming into him, by incessant repetition, the sanctity of the given order, thereby giving him the clearest possible picture of what is required of him and investing it with due ritual and the aura of ceremony and *mystique*. Then, in the moment of battle, the man will respond to that strong sense of discipline and duty, despite the infinitely great risk attaching to such a response. Courage is still required as resistance to the temptation to run away or to default; but it is made possible, or more possible, because it is set within this completely prepared framework.

This same principle is invariably present in the various episodes in the life of our Lord when courage is particularly evident. He did not attempt, as it were, to mobilize forces of courage in case an emergency should arise. He constantly rehearsed the will of God in His prayers and in His preaching so that the appropriate response to each challenge and temptation was clearly perceived in the light of that will. Herein lies the secret of that almost smooth and apparently effortless handling of ugly crowds and violent critics. Herein is the clue to the tranquillity of our Lord in the Judgement Hall and even under the whips and blows of the soldiers. His concentration was upon the things that God would have Him do, and this filled His mind and nerved His spirit. In the supreme test in the Garden of Gethsemane the natural revulsion against the agonies that awaited Him was immediately met by the thought of the Father's will, to which He had applied Himself so invariably that even in His critical hour that thought dominated His mind and fortified Him.

I find in St John's words, 'Father save me from this hour; but for this cause came I unto this hour', the inspired commentary on His spiritual struggle by one who, perhaps more than any other, was able to penetrate to its heart. 'Who would true valour see, let him come hither.'

As I think of the valour of Jesus, I am reminded all the while of the 'gentle Jesus meek and mild'. Much scorn has been thrown on this description of our Lord, and I shall have something to say about the 'meek and lowly' Jesus elsewhere in these pages. What is particularly relevant to our consideration of the courage of Jesus is the fact that courage has been divorced in the minds of many people today from any qualities of gentleness, and has been married to 'toughness' instead. The cult of 'aggressive masculinity', as it is politely called in the realm of the cinema, is a most insidious menace, particularly to adolescents. When we go to see a film, we are more likely than not to be bombarded with an efficient and absorbing display of violence in the expert hands of old favourites like James Cagney and Humphrey Bogart, and of others who will progressively take their place. At the moment, muscular morons who are, I believe, described in the language of Hollywood and Wardour Street as the 'cheese-cake boys' occupy this dubious stage. The intention lying behind this incessant emphasis on 'animal virility' is, of course, sexual, but to my mind the most dangerous of all the assumptions which it makes so persuasively is that courage is an expression of toughness or violence, and is indifferent to personal safety in the infliction of that violence on others. Understandably, this provides one of the clearest clues to the vexing problem of juvenile delinquency. The contempt for physical restraint as a mark of weakness, and the dubbing of all gentleness as 'cissy' are remarkable phenomena in every contemporary youth club and at every street corner. At its best, courage is devalued so that its worth is seen entirely in the physical realm; at its worst, it is perverted until it becomes a mixture of egotism and sadism. The war-cursed twentieth century has provided a sombre backcloth to this squalid degeneration of bravery, and has spawned all too many false heroes, who are held up to the susceptible gaze as models of behaviour.

What a corrective to all this is the courage of Jesus. He is that 'parfit gentil knight', to whom not even the most hostile critics have applied words like 'aggressive', or, that most objectionable of all epithets, 'he-man'. His manliness was not expressed in terms of muscle and biceps, but in the capacity to rise above the animal responses to danger and threats. He demonstrated on the Cross that human courage is essentially higher than animal courage. He repudiated violence instead of seeking to turn it against the threatener. In short, His was a spiritual quality which achieves its mastery only when it ceases to be masterful and combines with gentleness instead. When the High Priests tried to frighten Jesus, He did not try to frighten them in return; threat did not counter threat. When he was reviled, He reviled not again. It is not irreverent to think that He knew how precarious is a courage which relies on the body as its ally, for the body is treacherous and incalculable. He found the springs of resource and fortitude in the spirit; and as He speaks to me now from the Cross, He tells me that unless I too am ready to forsake the weapons of violence I cannot discover the higher qualities of heroism which are required of me as His disciple.

I see yet another aspect of the courage of Jesus in the light of my earliest thoughts of Jesus as a hero. The familiar appeal of His heroism, rather than of His Divine nature, was particularly effective when I was a growing boy. Jesus was presented to me as possessing all the virtues which I most admired but could not display. I came to think of Him as the one man who combined the highest qualities that filled my day-dreams, and I see now what a large place a sort of reckless dare-devil courage played in those day-dreams, and moreover how naturally I associated that quality with the heroic Jesus. I do not feel that I contracted much permanent harm from what I now see to have been a very imperfect conception of my Hero's valour. On the other hand, it is vitally necessary that this impression of reckless gallantry should be corrected. Meditation on the Passion of Jesus does provide that correction, at least for me. The courage of Jesus was not some kind of automatic reaction to the presence of danger or the appearance of evil.

There once lived in our house for some time a lordly Pekinese dog. It seemed to us that this small dog was fearless. A few doors away were four large spaniels who exercised themselves as a group. The mere sight of these spaniels sparked off in our Pekinese the most violent and valiant emotions. Without stopping to count the cost, which invariably was considerable, he would hurl himself at these comparatively innocent spaniels with a reckless abandon which was most exhilarating to watch—yet I hope, as you read this, that you feel a sense almost of bathos, because *that* kind of fearlessness has little, if anything, to do with the courage of our Lord. Heroism was a weapon He used sparingly. He recognized fear as a good thing in its appropriate place, which was that of a warning or a guide. He was not prepared to throw His life away in reckless abandon; He was only willing to give it away under the conditions where His bravery would produce the maximum results. That is surely why He avoided arrest in Galilee and said that it was inappropriate that a prophet should die outside Jerusalem. That is why He made no frontal attack upon the Roman power until He had used the opportunities that such power gave Him to propagate His message. That is why He told the parable of the wheat and the tares, and said: 'Let both grow together until the harvest.' Nothing is farther from the heroic temper of Jesus than the 'windmill tilting' of Don Quixote or the 'lashing out in all directions' of the threatened hero of my childhood dreams. He was neither reckless nor fearless. He counted the cost and then despised the shame. He felt the fear of death, and then at the decisive hour in the Garden He triumphantly opposed that fear with an indomitable spirit.

The Saviour who died on Calvary is for me the great exponent of courage, but He is much more than that. He is the great statesman of courage as well. He speaks to me of the bravery which is disciplined and canalized until it becomes the perfect instrument of power. Bertrand Russell defines power as 'the production of intended effects'. The spiritual valour of Jesus was the power upon which He was able to call to produce the effects which He intended. As I look at Him on the Cross, and hear His cry, 'It is finished, it is accomplished', I see the consummation of that intention. He had perceived with absolute clarity what His mission was, and He had been able to carry it out perfectly in the teeth of all that men could do to Him, because of His invincible courage. He is for me, and for all of us, the pattern, the polished diamond in its true setting, the pure courage of perfect manhood. 'Mighty Hero, strengthen me.'

THREE

Honesty

THERE are some virtues rare enough in men and women like ourselves which yet seem to shine so full-orbed in Jesus Christ that they are taken for granted when we think of Him. It seems almost an impertinence, for instance, to praise the honesty of Jesus Christ. Compared with the supreme virtues of perfect love and utter faithfulness, honesty may appear as the poor relation, but the reality is, upon examination, vastly different from its appearance. If honesty may be described as the most scrupulous care to avoid deceit, if it is the spotless observance of the command, 'Thou shalt not bear false witness', then the honesty of Jesus was the rarest of virtues in His own day, as dishonesty is one of the greatest curses of ours. In its most familiar form of lying, dishonesty (according to those most competent to speak) was deeply embedded in the character even of otherwise good men in Palestine nineteen hundred years ago. In the contacts that the Jew had with the foreigner, the merchant, the overlord, the servant and the slave, truthfulness was almost completely disregarded. 'To love your neighbour and to hate your enemy' meant not simply that you were entitled to do violence to your enemy, but that you were under no obligation to be honest with him either.

To put this principle from the other side—until it was established that the other man was your neighbour (and only a very few came within that restricted category) he could be treated as if he were an enemy. Therefore, over a wide field of human affairs and contacts, honesty was a work of super-erogation. There was nothing like a general obligation to be honest; and even now, a twentieth-century visitor to the Middle East will find no difficulty in accepting this statement as accurate. Maybe we who have inherited the non-conformist conscience still represent a standard in this matter which is higher than the general ethos of our contemporaries. It is clear that we have to attempt to think ourselves into a radically different world—a world of ubiquitous dishonesty—if we are to appreciate the honesty of our Lord.

Interestingly enough, there has been a significant example of this problem of adjustment in the conversations that recently took place between General Harding and Archbishop Makarios of Cyprus before the latter's deportation. Reading what reports have been made public of those negotiations brings to light the very great difference of approach to honesty between the two negotiators. The facile thing is to say that one was honest and the other dishonest. The wise thing is to recognize the clash of two vastly dissimilar moral codes—both of them, I think, sincerely held, but presenting truth from very different angles and with very different presuppositions.

The honesty of Jesus is a piercing light if seen against the brightest background, but it becomes the more dazzling when seen against the sombre background of His own day and His own people. The effort must be made to understand that background if His honesty is to speak to us with that compelling power with which, for instance, it spoke to Ignatius Loyola as he lay with a broken limb after the battle of Pampeluna.

I can still recapture the sense of amazement which accompanied my first more or less adult realization of the unity of our Lord's teaching as we have it in the Gospels. His words are so remarkably consistent. The extraordinary thing is not that there are variations in the records, and mutual contradictions as well, but that the broad outline of His teaching is not seriously affected by them. Despite the vastly different ways in which the authors of the various Gospels approach the words of Jesus, there is a consistency in the broad outline of those words which comes clearly down to us even in the translation of a translation. There are those who explain this consistency by claiming that the Holy Spirit of God guaranteed the Gospel-writers against error. This explanation of course falls to the ground if even the slightest error can be detected, and such errors must be plain even to the most

enthusiastic fundamentalist. In the light of assured scholarship, only invincible ignorance can be reconciled with literal
inspiration. Moreover, such an attitude obscures the invaluable fact that this consistency was there at the heart of our
Lord's message, and that honesty was the cement which held
each separate word of His together and built all those words up
into a majestic unity.

The forthrightness of what He had to say is admirably
caught and expressed by Luke in the record of the first acts in
the public ministry of our Lord. Luke tells us that immediately after the temptation in the wilderness—His Kingly
vigil—He came as His custom was into the Synagogue and read
a passage from Isaiah: 'The Spirit of the Lord is upon me,
because he hath anointed me to preach the gospel to the poor;
he hath sent me to heal the brokenhearted, to preach deliverance to the captives, and recovering of sight to the blind, to
set at liberty them that are bruised, to preach the acceptable
year of the Lord.' He closed the book, gave it back to the
attendant, and said: 'Today hath this scripture been fulfilled
in your ears.' This throwing down of the gauntlet, so to say,
without equivocation, simply and frankly, is the distinctive
mark of everything that followed. It explains the great
hostility of the Pharisees and the Sadducees. They knew
exactly where He stood and where in His eyes they had fallen
down. This is what is meant by the simple Gospel. No one
who pays careful attention to the Sermon on the Mount, for
example, would want to say that it was without intellectual
difficulties, that it was simple in the sense that a child could
understand its full meaning. The Gospel is simple in the
sense that its genuineness is not suspected, there are no
ulterior motives or degrees of sincerity to be reckoned with.
Listening to Jesus Christ is so vastly different from listening
to the best of ordinary men like ourselves. What we say has to
be assessed in the light of our vanity, or our calculated expediency, or our lapses from real sincerity, and this involves
complexity and uncertainty.

I turn to Jesus Christ, and in imagination sit at His feet
as He speaks, and there is immediately a restful simplicity. I

have no need to make allowances for the time and the place and the conditions under which He spoke this or that particular word. I can count on His unalterable honesty and can therefore give my full attention to what He says. That is what I mean by the simple gospel, and it is the fruit of His honesty.

When we say that the crucifixion of Jesus was not a sudden event that brought a catastrophic end to His life, but something implicit and foreshadowed from the day, at least, of His baptism, we are paying tribute again to the Saviour's honesty. He made clear the path that He would tread, and He did not swerve from it at any time or under any conditions. He made no attempt to accommodate the Gospel to any particular group or to revise the terms of discipleship to meet any awkward development. His honesty hastened His death, because His enemies were left in no doubt about the possibility of compromise and adjustment. The High Priests knew that each new day that dawned brought with it the same insistent demand from Jesus for a 'change of heart' on their part. Nothing was to be gained by delay—bargaining was out of the question—and the longer this man lived the more clearly and unmistakably His challenge rang out. There are but two courses to be taken with one who is quite incorruptible— accept Him or get rid of Him, for it is impossible to seduce Him or make use of Him. Whatever else we may say about the wickedness of His murderers, at least they acted logically and realistically from their own standpoint in killing Jesus as soon as they could.

Like His courage, this sheer honesty, this absolute frankness of Jesus, made its powerful impact on the minds and in the hearts of those who played their various parts in the final drama of His Passion. Much has been said and written about the character of Pontius Pilate, although the amount of evidence upon which any general estimate of his character can be reached is scanty and almost contradictory. We may safely assume, however, that as a Roman colonial governor he was not himself interested in the religious ideas of those whom he governed in Jerusalem. With their religious practices he was much more familiar, and he had from time to time to take

careful account of them. Especially was it his concern, on
pain of disgrace, or recall at least, to see to it that those
religious practices did not threaten the 'Pax Romana'. He
knew well enough that there was a more militant wing of
Jewish resistance, and that spasmodic 'resistance groups' could
blaze very quickly into serious rebellion unless they were
ruthlessly crushed. It seems reasonable, therefore, to infer
that when Jesus was first brought before him, Pilate's only
clear thought was probably that here was yet another who was
trying to stir up the people. Maybe upon examination many
such who had been brought before him had protested their
innocence and non-violent intentions. The striking fact is that
Jesus made Pilate believe it.

It cannot have been the force of our Lord's teaching which
convinced Pilate. The most enlightened officer of Rome would
have been almost impervious to teaching, even when confronted with the spiritual genius of such a prisoner, and Pilate
showed no signs of especial spiritual insight. The simple
explanation is surely the best one—Pilate was staggered out of
his routine indifference by the complete honesty of his prisoner.
In the midst of intrigue and double-dealing, here was one man
who spoke the truth as He saw it, and nothing but the truth.
Pilate did his best to save an honest man, and only when the
blackmailing accusation that he was not Caesar's friend was
flung at him, did this comparatively decent Roman give way
and escape as best he could from His penetrating eyes and
fling Him to the wolves.

We ought to look with keen attention at this quality in
Jesus, not only because it is a rare virtue, but also because
today honesty is not one of the attributes most usually credited
to the Christian Church or its members. There are many who
feel that intellectual integrity is no longer zealously guarded
by the followers of Jesus. They do not bleakly accuse us of
Jesuitry, or suggest that we justify the means by the end
(and let me add that the Order of Jesus is on the whole quite
unjustly saddled with this accusation); what they feel is that
in our enthusiasm for results, in the zest for conversions for
example, the strict adherence to truth is less important than

the appeal to the heart. 'Get a man converted first—theology comes afterwards' is one way in which this emphasis is expressed. I find this most perilous and, in the open-air, destructive of all confidence in the evangelist. I remember being warned by my theological Principal, Dr Maldwyn Hughes, that a preacher is never justified in telling his flock for the good of its soul what can be demonstrated to be untrue. Now, after thirty years, I feel that the most damaging accusation that can be levelled at Christians is that we are less honest in our pulpits than scientists are in their laboratories or teachers in their classrooms. It may be that cynicism is the residuary legatee of two world wars; certainly it is profoundly disconcerting to find how many of the young people on the fringe of the Church think of us as taking part in a kind of harmless racket—kidding ourselves along with impossible dogmas and bearing amiable false witness in the interests of peace and goodwill. In particular, the use of the slogan 'The Bible says' is dishonest. I appreciate the contention of certain theologians that it is possible to discover in the Bible an underlying unity which runs like a golden thread through its many different pages. But I do not believe this in any objective, scientific sense. It is at best a feeling which we read into the document rather than a fact which we read out of it. Except in the sense that it is all about God, the Bible to me has no simple unity of thought or purpose. However, whether I am right or wrong about that, it is certainly true that the Bible says almost anything you want it to say, according to the place at which you decide to open it.

I am not concerned in these pages to attempt an evaluation of the Bible. I am anxious to bring home to the conscience of the reader, that an evangelism which uses this statement as a text, and indeed as a bludgeon, stands condemned before the honesty of its Lord. The nemesis that follows is that when once the preacher has been caught out in a bit of fervent insincerity his credibility has gone, and he will see no fruit of his preaching among those who have a regard for the truth. I remember the verse in the *Methodist Sunday School Hymnbook*—'Those who have deceived, Even when they

speak the truth will not be believed'. How terribly true that is.
I often feel that a transformation would take place in the
Churches if some—not all, I admit, but some—of the things
we parsons say at our fraternal gatherings, and around our
own hearth fires, we were prepared to say in our pulpits also.

Let me then come to the Cross and learn again of my Lord's
honesty, for without it I cannot be His witness and am not
really fit to call myself by His name.

As I think about this unswerving integrity of the Master, I
feel that perhaps the greatest difference between His attitude to
truth and my own, when I am at my best, lies in our differing
assessments of the power of honesty. Jesus had a complete
respect for truthfulness. He believed that it was potent in itself,
that it was a dynamic thing which produced liberty and must
finally prevail. Like wisdom for the later Jewish prophets, like
logos for St John, truthfulness for Him was active power. I,
on the other hand, tend to a much more academic and passive
idea of truthfulness. I want to bolster it with diplomacy and to
protect it from being misunderstood. 'You can't tell the truth
to a man with a cancer which he believes to be only indigestion.
It will do no good, and in fact will do a great deal of harm to tell
him the truth; so deceive him for his own good.' So runs the
familiar argument. I feel the power of it and am sure that
there are times when silence is better than speech anyhow.
But when something must be said, is complete honesty the
right road to take?

At the foot of the Cross I am sure it is. Jesus tells me that
it is a kind of arrogance to think that honesty is only practicable
when the results of that honesty can be foreseen and, moreover, foreseen to be satisfactory. Truthfulness is not an
occasional virtue or a seasonal task. The testimony of Jesus is
that it is always better to risk telling the truth than to risk
withholding it.

In my own ministerial experience I have proved that in every
case where I feared to tell a sufferer the truth about his
condition, but then conquered that fear and, with reticence,
but with frankness, resisted the temptation to deceive him,
the result was remarkable. I found that my fears were largely

groundless, and that the sufferer seemed much better able to absorb a distressing truth than to accept an unconvincing lie. In short, honesty was the best policy.

I marvel at the tranquillity of Jesus, the complete absence of fluster. He was never taken off His guard and seldom involved in the necessity of making a second statement to explain a first. I compare this composure with my own fret, and I am sure that part of the secret of His security was that He was never afflicted by the problem of reconciling His words with one another. He could not be quoted against Himself, and even when He was, as at His trial, the accusation of 'destroying the Temple' was so patently absurd that it was quickly dropped. I remember a likeable rascal I once knew in Pentonville Prison. He said to me in a moment of candour: 'The trouble with telling lies is that you've got to have such a good memory.' Exactly! And what a blessed comfort it is to find how entirely an honest man is relieved of the trouble of having to try to remember what he said before. It removes the tension and in a remarkable way makes life easier. This is one meaning, among many, in the invitation which Jesus extends to each of us to 'Take My yoke upon you and learn of Me, for My yoke is easy and My burden is light'. The burden of the Christian life carried in integrity, and the witness to our Lord made in honesty, will not chafe. Honesty, as its meaning is, makes the Christian life straightforward.

Before leaving this matter of our Lord's honesty, I would add something more to what has already been said about reticence. To my thinking, the undisciplined John Blunt kind of honesty is a crippled virtue, and is disagreeable to boot. It is not the fact that I come from the 'soft south' rather than from the harder north which persuades me that John Blunt is an objectionable character; it is the fact that honesty is better spoken quietly than shouted at the top of the voice. I find nothing amiable at all in the man who prides himself that 'he speaks his mind and doesn't care who knows it'. Integrity never needs rudeness to make it effective, and those who in the interests of straightforwardness remain indifferent to the feelings of their fellows are making an unworthy exhibition of their professed integrity, rather than making a witness to the truth. If they would examine their motives with due care they would find that egotism plays as large a part in their make-up as honesty. It is not enough to tell the truth; we are to tell it in love, as Jesus did. Here, as ever, He was in all His ways most wonderful. He spoke the truth for our sakes, and not in order to call attention to His own respect for it. His own truthfulness shone the more luminously for that very reason. At His trial, the testimony of Jesus was enough to establish His own attitude. There was no hesitation and no ambiguity in His words, but there was reticence and self-discipline. How careful He was not to inflame the proceedings by the kind of 'speech from the dock' to which we are so much accustomed in political trials today.

The parade of honesty, the aggressive, provocative blurting out of the truth—these things have no place whatsoever in the make-up of Jesus Christ, and nowhere is this quiet sincere truthfulness so potent as in His last hours. It is not claimed for the Passion records that they contain a full transcript, for instance, of the trials of Jesus before the Chief Priest and before Pilate. They, like all the other records, have pre-eminently a didactic quality. 'These things are written that ye may believe, and that believing ye may have life in his name.' Nevertheless, the terseness itself of the record of His trial is surely intended to draw attention to the stringent economy of words which Jesus Himself preserved. And there is a lesson there for me, and probably for a great many others; it is that honesty is often over-emphasized in wordy speech, because it is under-emphasized in action. It may well be that 'protesting too much' is the revealing symptoms in the Church life of today of the gaping abyss that stretches between our many brave words and our few good actions.

I find that the honesty of Jesus pierces me like the thrust of a knife. Perhaps others are not afflicted, as I seem to be, with the temptation to hedge and adapt and adulterate the truth. How desperately hard I often find it to say exactly what I know I ought to say when a particular member of the Church is sitting facing me, and when a special friend will violently disagree. I was so much afflicted by this sort of temptation at one time that I was driven to an expedient which I feel would not be entirely condemned by God. I removed my glasses so that I could not see my congregation, except as a 'sinful blur', and then I had freedom in preaching. I have discovered since, in a hard school, that honesty is not only required of the speaker, in the open-air for instance, but also that it is the only way to hold the respect of the crowd. Best of all, it is a sure way of bringing home to the sceptic at least one of the Christian truths—that this is the sort of world which is the better for honesty and the worse for deceit. Though this may sound trite, I wonder whether it would be given house-room in men's minds had it not been for the Son of Man who came to make us free in the fellowship of His truthfulness.

FOUR

Meekness

IF there is one quality in the character of Jesus which, to put it at its lowest, has outstanding publicity value, it is meekness. The 'meek and lowly' Jesus has fascinated even the most hostile critics of Christian morality, and has evoked the adoring love of Christian saints. From the scholarly Hindu mystic, like one who talked to me in Ceylon, to the casual pagan who takes a dilettante interest in religious affairs (and I meet him every week in the open-air), this meekness of Jesus is regarded as perhaps His especial moral characteristic. It is beloved by the best, as well as by the more sentimental, hymn-writers, so that its theme is constantly upon the lips of Church people. It makes its own particular appeal to children, and it is the quality which more than any other shines through the Crucifixion story.

It is not difficult to understand the popularity that Christ's meekness has attained, because it is more easily read off from the Gospels than are His other virtues, and the reason for this is not far to seek. Superficially, at least, meekness is one of the easiest of His virtues for the Gospel writers to describe, and the evidences and illustrations of it are prolific, as compared, for example, with what we are told about His moral purity.

The physical and economic setting of our Lord's life suggests meekness, although those who live in such circumstances are not necessarily meek. He was born in poverty, and unfortunately the poor have always been expected to combine a suitable humility with their penury. In biblical times, humility before their superiors in class and wealth was the approved and almost universal attitude of the poor and lowly, and who would dare to deny that in many places in the modern world this condition still persists? In the eyes, therefore, of His social contemporaries, the fact that Jesus was born of a peasant woman and laid in a manger set the pattern for His subsequent ministry. It was a pattern in which there was neither privilege nor the kind of pride that attached itself to the high-born. Instead of panoply and splendour, His surrounding circumstances were those of poverty and indignity. His entourage in His public ministry was a band of fishermen, and apart from Judas, who may have been high born, and who almost certainly was a man of unusual calibre, Jesus moved among the common people and only occasionally had contact with men of substance like Nicodemus and Lazarus. All this is familiar knowledge.

What is not so familiar, maybe, is the way in which these conditions predisposed His hearers to an acceptance of what they imagined this message of humility to be. In very many ways they had taken a form of meekness into their general attitude and outlook. Theologically, the Hebrew, who thought in terms of sacrifice as the necessary method of approach to God, and went on to think of the animal sacrifice of a lamb, could not but think also of the meekness of this least aggressive and violent of all creatures. One of the great central strains in Hebrew thought was about one who would be the 'Lamb of God', and in Isaiah this teaching was expressed in terms of defencelessness and docility. Those who thought of Jesus as in any way fulfilling this hope, or even claiming to do so, remembered the 'lamb that before her shearers was dumb' and believed that the Lamb of God was much more the uncomplaining victim than the stalwart champion.

Again, nationally, the Hebrew of our Lord's day lived in a concentration camp. Palestine was an occupied country; and it is fascinating to realize that many of the contemporary situations in our Western world can be paralleled almost exactly in the Galilee and Jerusalem of the first century. There were resistance leaders like Judas the Gaulonite, Quislings like Herod, Gauleiters like Pilate, petty collaborators like Matthew, and terrorists like Barrabas. There was all the apparatus of the police State, and paradoxically all the tolerance which from time to time accompanies immense tyrannies. Moreover, there were in Palestine two fundamentally opposite attitudes to the occupying power, just as there were in France from 1940 to 1945. Some, like the de Gaullists, proclaimed a policy of underground violence, and others preached a policy of acquiescence and near acceptance.

In this political field the meekness of Jesus seemed to fit naturally into the already existing categories. It was not difficult, for instance, for those who listened to Jesus to make up their minds that He was totally opposed to the underground resistance groups. They naturally thought of Him as belonging to the other group. In the political field the meekness of Jesus appeared to be quite a simple and recognizable interpretation of the technique of one who would have no part in sabotage or rebellion. The important point about all this is that in a land of violence, where it might well have been thought that ideas of passive resistance were unheard of, and that pacifists were non-existent, the contrary turns out to be the case.

Socially, religiously, and politically a certain type of meekness or of non-resistance was both well known and widely practised. Whether or not this was the Christlike virtue we call meekness is a matter for discussion in these pages. The immediately relevant fact is that here a climate of opinion was already impregnated with something that was at any rate associated with meekness. Whatever else the disciples and the Pharisees did not understand about Jesus, they at least thought they understood His humility. It would seem to me, therefore, that to interpret the opposition from the Priests and the Zealots to Jesus as being the result of His general attitude to non-violent resistance is unprofitable. It was surely the announcement He made that such meekness would lead to a gibbet, and not to an earthly triumph, which they found impossible to believe or respect.

It is easy to see why the militant underground rejected Jesus out of hand. He would lend Himself to none of their plans. Embedded in the reason for which the other group rejected Him is, finally, the key to the perfidy and tragedy of the Cross. I will not, then, write about the many illustrations in the Gospel of the gentleness and kindly modesty of the

Saviour, but will try to share with others who may read these words the sense of quite revolutionary meekness which Jesus displayed—a meekness that was misunderstood by His enemies and most of His friends, and that has similarly been misunderstood ever since.

Jesus was completely without the deadliest of all sins— pride. Here is a great secret. Taking Dr Temple's definition of pride as 'putting yourself where only God has a right to be' it is not difficult to see how egocentric is so much that the Hebrews and we call meekness. The humble poor are historically seldom humble at all. I gladly put on record my own experience in meeting poor people who have been marvellous in their humility and lovely in their unaffected gentleness; I have known the 'poor in spirit' who have already inherited the Kingdom of Heaven. But as a rule poverty goes with bitterness and resentment, or else with cringing and subservience. Only the spiritual giants can overcome the terrible curse of poverty, and most human beings are far from being giants. Ninety per cent of you who may read this would fall victims either to subservience or to hate if you had to live in the same way as the peasants of our Lord's time. The overwhelming effect of poverty is to condemn its victims to an existence where 'self-preservation' becomes the dominant, if almost hopeless, theme. Among the many stimuli I received from reading Bernard Shaw was the appreciation of the truth lying behind his repeated assertion that poverty is a crime. That is, of course, an exaggeration, like nearly everything Shaw said; a man who is poor is not thereby a criminal. But grinding poverty is overwhelmingly bad in its effects; it is a forcing bed of evil. I am glad that I read Shaw before I read Marx, for he prepared my mind so that I was able to bring some critical faculty to Marx's materialistic and determinitive dogmas. I reject, with indignation, the Communistic claim that spiritual values are a superstructure erected upon a material foundation which is essentially economic; but I whole-heartedly concur with the judgement that the proletarian, as the unprivileged member of a class-ridden society, is largely moulded by the evil conditions which he endures. In particular his poverty breeds a certain kind of self-interest; he is driven in upon himself. He is compelled to the belief that he must look, as it were, outside himself for his deliverance, and yet at the same time he must cultivate the class-conscious confidence in his capacity, along with his fellow-sufferers, to break out of his prison and claim his rightful place in the world. As you know, the Communist Manifesto ends with the ringing words: 'Proletarians of all lands, unite! You have only your chains to lose and a world to gain.' Whether you agree with this battle cry or not, there can be no doubt about the motive which informs it; it is a mixture of selfishness and pride and self-confidence.

The particular point I am making in this context is that the non-violent poor of our Lord's day were nevertheless ideologically (I knew that word would appear sooner or later) the products, in part, of their poverty-stricken conditions, and whether or not they were passive and cringing and subservient in practice, in their hearts there was pride and violence. In absolute contrast to this conditioned reaction to poverty and oppression was the selfless meekness of Jesus. For Him salvation lay not in the cultivation of the class interest of the group to which one belongs, but in the humble denial of one's selfish rights in the search for the common good. This is what makes nonsense of the attempts made by Marxists today to appropriate Jesus Christ as a sort of tame revolutionary in their Marxist Pantheon. Once again, this selfless humility of Jesus is, for me, seen in its quintessence when He came to His death.

Before the triumph of Mao Tse-tung over Chiang Kai-shek on China's mainland, there were many Communist martyrs. Missionary friends of mine have told me how some of them died up against a wall, and how they hurled their defiance at their killers even at the moment of death. 'Long live the Revolution! We are dying now, but your turn will come—you may kill us, but we shall prevail. We deny you and denounce you.' Such are typical examples. In courage and integrity they bore their cross like Jesus, but in the spirit of their dying how different they were from Him. Jesus at His trial

bore testimony unflinchingly to the triumph of God's Kingdom and of the Son of Man, but He prayed for the forgiveness
of His murderers, and apart from His cries of thirst and of
desolation, it was the salvation of the world for which He
agonized. He fulfilled His own words spoken months before
in His public ministry: 'If any man will come after me let him
deny himself and take up his cross.' His meekness was perfect
submission to God, in which He was Himself perfectly at rest.

Full of egotism as I am, I can yet see the meaning of those
words of the German hymn-writer:

> *O Jesus Christ, grow Thou in me,*
> *And all things else recede:*
> *My heart be daily nearer Thee*
> *From sin be daily freed*

Such is the humility that has completely emancipated itself
from the ties of circumstance, and that for ever gives the lie
to economic determinism.

In the theological, as in the social realm, I am convinced, as
I stand at the foot of the Cross, of the profound difference
between the idea of meekness that the Jew associated with a
sacrificial lamb and the quality of meekness displayed by our
Lord. Mark Twain, one of the greatest of wits, is reported to
have entitled a description of Queen Victoria's Diamond
Jubilee, which he made for a New York daily paper: 'Blessed
are the meek, for they shall inherit the earth.' The irony is
magnificent, but so is the insight. Mark Twain, for all the
inadequacies of his own personal character, was in no doubt
that meekness is a positive virtue and not just the absence of
aggressiveness, and he was sardonically calling attention to the
British Empire as the product of this virtue.

It is this positive nature of meekness that Jesus stresses,
rather than the negative submissiveness of a lamb led to the
slaughter. For Jesus, and therefore for us, meekness is active,
not passive, it is a constructive attitude to evil which has its
own dynamic technique. The 'Pale Galilean' as an ineffective
object of our pity is a grotesque cartoon that has misled men
and women and has perverted the humility of Jesus out of all

recognition. It must be with a sense of astonishment that those who read a Gospel, after having seen such a cartoon of our Lord's character, find the record of an aggressive rather than a regressive person. That aggressiveness was entirely free from violence and malice, but it was characteristic of Him at all times. To use the imagery of the battlefield (and as a pacifist I do not see why the supporters of violence should have all the best illustrations), Jesus took the war into the enemy's country. His strategy was offensive, and His tactics to bring that enemy to action. Where others confided in swords and spears, Jesus bade His disciples go empty-handed on their evangelistic mission, and promised them that their very helplessness would overcome more opposition than ever swords could achieve. The triumphant entry into Jerusalem was the superb public gesture He made to the power of meekness. The Cross was the final battle which He fought with meekness, and suffering was the weapon with which he gained the victory. Jesus was indeed gentle and mild, but those traits in no way conflicted with the dynamic thrust of His assault upon the strongholds of evil. There was no inconsistency between His passive resistance to the soldiers who tortured Him and His forthright attacks upon the Pharisees who opposed His Kingdom.

To see how Christlike meekness distinguishes between 'amour propre' and 'righteous indignation' is, for me, to arrive at the heart of the matter. Jesus was free to denounce His enemies, to make unbridled condemnation of the sins of others, because He was entirely indifferent to personal prestige. I dare not ascribe righteous indignation to myself, because of the self-interest that stains my motives. I am not meek enough for my goodness to cut like a sword into the evils of others. The word 'unbridled' has come to be used in a pejorative sense precisely because, when we sinners give full rein to our condemnation of sin, we lose control of ourselves. We are not meek enough to be wholehearted in condemnation. Like so many other truths about our Saviour, this truth must be caught rather than taught, and these words of mine are poor things. I remember Dr Percy Dearmer commenting on what he said was the greatest hymn for Palm Sunday, and one of the genuine lyrics of the Passion. He pointed out how the writer had captured the dynamic majesty of Christ's humility. I agree with Dr Dearmer, for the lines bring one closer to its meaning than any of these foregoing words of mine. Here they are:

> *Ride on, ride on in majesty!*
> *In lowly pomp ride on to die;*
> *Bow Thy meek head to mortal pain,*
> *Then take, O God, Thy power, and reign.*

These reflections on the meekness of Jesus would be incomplete and even academic unless some attention was given to the particular application of this quality which is associated with the word pacifism. This is not a book about pacifism, but there is not much point in talking about the meekness of Jesus without commenting on His attitude to violence as an instrument for the achievement of personal and social ends. I will give my own testimony in this matter rather than seek to present an argument. As I try to understand the words of Jesus recorded in the Gospels by looking at them in the light of His actions, I have the quite overwhelming sense that Jesus rejected any form of violence as an instrument of His Kingdom. That was the recurring pattern in His preaching and the effect He produced upon both His friends and His enemies. Let me put it this way. I find it impossible to think of Jesus taking any part in His own day in military activities even with the highest of objectives. To give Jesus any sort of uniform and to put any sort of weapon, ancient or modern, into His hands is for me an incredible thought. Jesus makes Himself known to each of us as we make our own various attempts to get into touch with Him, by reading about Him, by praying, by talking, by imagining. Quite apart, at the moment, from the practical considerations of pacifism, Jesus, as a person, confronts me with the unique challenge of a life in which the use of violence had no place whatsoever. I cannot necessarily see how that refusal to use any kind of coercion would work in some particular condition or emergency, but I know that the outward and visible sign of His meekness was that He would do no violence. I often have doubts about this tremendous venture of non-resisting love in a violent world, but I am strengthened at the foot of the Cross and my faith in Him is confirmed there. The Cross of Jesus is the instrument of our salvation. Jesus seems to me to confront the sin of the world with a suffering love which is not only an offering to God—a sufficient sacrifice for the sins of the world—but a plan for its salvation, and a strategy for peace and goodwill.

It is possible to argue that the repudiation of all forms of violence, from the hangman's rope to the Hydrogen Bomb, is an impossible programme that could only be carried through by the Son of God. It is not possible, I think, to make sense of our Saviour's life and work until it is recognized that such repudiation was what his meekness implied. At any rate, such is my experience. And to that I must also add something more. I have read carefully in the literature of the primitive Christian Church, and I am reasonably convinced that these first Christian communities were pacifist because pacifism was the obvious exposition for them of the spirit of their risen Lord. The taking of life, being involved in coercive political action, the business of soldiering, were proscribed for—or rather were not even considered by—men and women who were trying to walk in the footsteps of Christ. I find that Heering in his book *The Fall of Christianity* makes out a fully documented and unanswerable case for the constructive objection of the early Church to all forms of war and warlike action. I also find it impossible to disagree with the title of his book. Christianity has fallen from grace and from effective power because it has departed from the meek spirit of its Founder.

When I hear Jesus say to me 'Take up your cross and follow Me', I must free my hands so that I may hold that cross. I cannot hold the cross while my fist is clenched. I cannot hold the cross if I am already grasping a sword. I cannot hold the cross so long as I insist that I must have also in my hand a written understanding that assures its success. There is a kind of nakedness that belongs to meekness and cross-bearing. I think of these things and, as I think, I look at Jesus on the Tree, and I realize that words are poor things. I wish I had that strange and wonderful gift to suggest by words great spiritual insights, so that the words themselves become the breath and finer spirit of knowledge; but suddenly I remember other familiar words that light up with new and creative meaning. I need not grope for words; let me ponder the truth as it is in Jesus, and I shall find at the end of my thinking that God has put into the mind of one of His children the words I would frame, but cannot, and I shall take His words for my thoughts, and see in them new and profound meaning.

Toplady wrote:

> *Nothing in my hands I bring,*
> *Simply to Thy cross I cling.*

I have sung these words many times and have thought as I have sung them of my unworthiness and my inability to bring any gifts to my Lord. I do not know what dominant thought was in Toplady's mind as he wrote them. I do know that, thinking of the meekness of Jesus, these words have sprung to new life for me. It is the Saviour who emptied Himself of all but love who calls to me from His Cross to empty myself of pride and violence so that I may be able to wield the cross as I carry it.

FIVE

Hopefulness

WHEN challenged by the great Christian virtues, as they are to be seen in Jesus, I have often felt a somewhat impudent optimism with regard to one of them —hope. Faith, love, purity, honesty, loom before me as spiritual peaks, sublime to contemplate and infinitely difficult to scale, but I have often thought that I could tackle hope. Compared with these other tremendous mountains of goodness, is not hope rather like a foothill, pleasant to view and easy to climb. If I cannot at this moment enjoy God's Kingdom, what hinders me from at least hoping for it? If I cannot love my enemy I can at least hope that he will one day cease to be an enemy. If the record of my own pilgrimage is at best a series of desultory forays in the spiritual world, and at worst a series of miserable failures, yet does not hope 'spring eternal'? Only where there is effort is there honesty, but 'while there is life there is hope'.

Such reflections almost persuade me that hope has no justifiable place alongside faith and love in the triumvirate of graces. In fact I tend to question whether it is a virtue at all in the same sense that purity is. Yet the early Christian Church had no doubt whatsoever about the nature of hope as a necessary element in a Christian's character. Paul's references to hope are frequent and familiar. More important still, they indicate what a central place it plays, in his judgement, in the Christian life. One has only to call to mind the passage in Romans 8[24]: 'For we are saved by hope: but hope that is seen is not hope: for what a man seeth, why doth he yet hope for? But if we hope for that we see not, then do we with patience wait for it.' Such a passage (and it could be matched with many others) disposes of the contention that hope for a Christian is just another form of faith or of trust. It further disposes of the idea that hope is nothing more than the fervour with which we entertain other virtues, such as single-mindedness or courage.

Hope for the first Christians and throughout the Christian era has been much more than a 'contingent quality of optimism' giving a bloom and a radiance to the grim qualities of endurance and sacrificial love. Paul obviously thinks of hope as one specific item in the whole armour of God which the Christian must put on: 'Put on for a helmet', says he, 'the hope of salvation.' What he does not say is 'let your helmet glint with hope'.

I think that perhaps the moment at which I first felt constrained to reconsider this quality of hope—to re-examine the somewhat easy assumptions I had made about it—was upon first reading *Pilgrim's Progress*. In particular, the tremendous description of Pilgrim's crossing the river, supported by the strong arms of Hope as his final companion, made a great impression, not only upon my emotions but also upon my mind. I experienced that sudden sense of 'Rightness'. I felt that Bunyan's insight was right, that it was entirely appropriate that Pilgrim's journey should be completed in this way, and that but for the strong arms of Hope, Christian would have drowned even within sight of his goal.

So I turn again to Jesus as He is portrayed in the Gospels, and especially in His Passion, and I find that it is possible to separate from His other characteristics a buoyancy of spirit, a quality of persistent cheerfulness, that becomes the more obvious as I look at it. Jesus is the supreme exponent of that attitude to life which is called 'world embracing' in contrast to the attitude described as 'world renouncing'. These two phrases are familiar as the ones most frequently associated with the great world religions. Buddhism is essentially a 'world renouncing' faith. Its goal is the annihilation of desire of all kinds, and though western critics of Buddhism have been too facile in asserting that Nirvana is the state of nothingness, it is not inaccurate to insist that hope has no place among Buddhist virtues. Christianity, on the other hand, is 'world embracing'. Its goal is the realization of God's realm—a dominion of which is to be found on this earth, while the motherland is a non-material Kingdom beyond. Whatever convictions may be held about the world being lost, the Christian hope is that it may be found again.

I suppose to most people living in this country the optimistic background to Christianity is taken more or less for granted. We are 'world embracing' by tradition and circumstance and temper. But one has only to take some interest in Barthian thinking on the continent of Europe, and to talk optimistically of the future to displaced Europeans who have undergone the ravages of two world wars, to appreciate how local this optimism really is. Our hopefulness is in the air we breathe— it is what seems natural to us. Surely that is why its virtue, when expressed by Jesus, is difficult to realize. Latvians, East Germans, Alsatians, and men and women who have lived their lives in continuous bondage in one D.P. camp and another, are amazed at such cosmic cheerfulness. To them the cheerfulness of Jesus, who lived in circumstances far nearer their own than ours, is remarkable; in fact it is so remarkable that European theologians of the Barthian persuasion have felt compelled to separate that cheerfulness from the historical process, as they see it, in order to preserve it from what they would otherwise regard as its inevitable fate—incredibility.

Again, this optimistic attitude to life in general, and to the prospects for humanity in particular, is not only a local phenomenon; it is a recent one as well. I have been much impressed, in reading Bertrand Russell's *History of Western Philosophy*, by the point he makes, that until comparatively recent times in the western world, all thinking was about death. The ubiquity of death as a fact and as a threat is strange to us, even though we have passed through two world wars in fifty years. I will not speak of soldiers on battlefields, because I have never been one of them, but I remember vividly being a civilian under bombardment from the air, both in 1914-18 and 1939-45. I was regularly frightened, and often cheek by jowl with immediate and mortal danger, but I did not expect to be killed. As far as I know, neither did any of my fellow citizens, although many of them were killed. My thoughts were upon the life I could lead when these dangers were past—not on the world to which I should go when my life was taken —and Bertrand Russell reminds me that this mental temper is modern and unprecedented and, of course, in many events unreasonable.

Poverty, disease, natural disaster, wars—these were the conditions under which man was driven to see his life as short, if not brutish. Only the few lived to old age, and their advancing years were marked by the passing, one by one, of their kinsfolk and acquaintances. Most people who thought at all applied their hope to another world, because it was a forlorn thing in this one. This should not be taken to mean that they were necessarily miserable. The opposite of hopefulness is hopelessness, not misery.

Trevelyan, in his *English Social History*, makes a good case for the comparative happiness of many simple people living in England in the days of Elizabeth I. They were not plagued by the frustration of false hopes any more than they were unduly encouraged by the presence of real ones. They just lived without hope and made the best of what they thought was a bad job. They made friends with death, because that was the only company they could keep. In a way they were cheerful; it would be absurd to deny it. There were indeed in the Renaissance spirit, out of which came the marvellous blossoming of Elizabethan art, the beginnings of that hope which had been so long repressed or lost and of which we are the heirs today; but the important distinction seems to me to be that the optimism of people who lived in the constant presence of death was either a confidence by faith in a future life or an unquenchable *joie de vivre*, and neither of these qualities is identical with the Christian virtue of hope as it is seen in Jesus.

From the very first, the story of Jesus is set in the midst of the 'Messianic Hope'. Jesus was born among people who lived by looking forward, and who awaited the good time that was coming. Moreover, Jesus had become for the Christian Church the risen and triumphant Saviour by the time the Gospels were written. That the Gospels should be invested with a radiance of unquenchable hope is therefore what we should expect; and we cannot be surprised to find it there, even though Jesus was rejected by His own people. What is outstanding, however, is the note of hopefulness that is constantly sounded by the One who Himself identified His Messianic role with suffering love. The reader of the New Testament willl look in vain for any suggestion of melancholy in the character of our Lord. He will also look in vain for effervescence. What he will find is buoyancy. Jesus lived His life under the Cross, but never 'under the weather', and when He finally came to that Cross, with its pain and loneliness, His hope held Him up.

I suggest that this distinction between ebullience and buoyancy is an important one. I have a strong personal dislike for what is called 'heartiness', and a still stronger objection to the contention that a Christian should be 'hearty'. Nothing is more exhausting than the kind of cheerfulness which seems to contain a maximum of aggressiveness with a minimum of restraint. Those who claim that, being soundly converted, they are now 'happy all the day' leave me intellectually and emotionally cold, especially when this happiness tends to express itself in a perpetual grin. There is a world of difference between a faith which persuades you to laugh your head off with optimism and one which enables you to hold your head up with confidence. It is precisely here that the wonderful equanimity of Jesus provides not only a correction but also the norm. Jesus went to His Cross in sorrow and in much disappointment. As I watch Him there, I see hope as the virtue which blends with sorrow and disappointment and makes them creative, not merely pitiful. God will give to me, as He gave to Jesus, such hope as will turn my sorrow, when it comes, into a channel of blessing to others, just as the sorrow of our Lord becomes a challenge to those who see it. Without hope, disappointment is a pathetic thing that begets cynicism at the last. With hope, disappointment is a spur to effort, a wrong to be righted, and a call to fresh and greater endeavour.

So the indomitable spirit of Jesus makes His disappointment at the perfidy of His friends a positive challenge to those same friends. In like manner, if I have a steadfast hope, God will take the disappointments that come to me in my very imperfect life, and will turn them into occasions of new achievement. That and more is what the hope of Jesus says to me. On the Cross this hopefulness was an achievement of the will over the body and the emotions. I tread warily in the field of relationship between the body and the feelings, and I have no word of psychological dogma to offer on this theme. What is abundantly clear is that Jesus accepted the plain duty of the believer in God to practise cheerfulness at all times. In other words, Christian hope springs from the will rather than from the natural conditions of a believer's life, and less still from his feelings. Jesus, even while dying, allowed Himself no respite from this unceasing obligation to witness to hope. It was a superb victory of the will over a physical misery which must have exercised an almost overwhelming effect upon His feelings as well.

By this determined hope, Jesus, to use a somewhat prosaic phrase, maintained the initiative, and, to use a cumbrous one, determined the psychological climate in which He faced His enemies. For me this is the heart of hope. It is the virtue of wilful cheerfulness, indomitability, resilience. How I wish there were a good Anglo-Saxon word to describe it. There isn't, but there is a French one—the Christian who achieves hope becomes 'debonair', he possesses 'the good air'. He refuses to allow any circumstances of evil or of distress to reduce him to lethargy. Whatever he feels he will still 'put on a good courage' as a man puts on an overcoat, so that he can go out into the fiercest and most biting winds. Hope, even in the worst and most disheartening circumstances, will assure him that he is still, by this very grace itself, the captain of his soul.

Moreover, hope is the virtue which preserves the freedom of the Christian when in almost every sense the Christian's freedom of action is curtailed to the point of extinction. Jesus was nailed to a piece of wood. His body was in chancery. His enemies had destroyed His physical freedom; they had from a temporal point of view overridden His ministry. It may well

be, as I have indicated elsewhere, that even His mental freedom was temporarily impaired by the torture of crucifixion.
What they could not do was to prevent the exercise of His
freedom to hope, and it was through this culvert, which even
the agonies of the Cross could not close, that grace flowed
unceasingly and the spiritual contact between Jesus and His
Father was maintained.

Thus the picture of Hope becomes clearer to me the nearer
I draw to Calvary. I would still think that as a virtue it eludes
the closer kind of definition, yet, for me, it grows in importance and in significance in the sombre light of the crucifixion.
More vital still, it presents itself as a persistent challenge to the
will of the would-be Christian. If faith is a gift of God, it is a
gift made to the would-be believer who in his own power
practises the virtue of hope. I am challenged here and now,
while I await such grace as will enable me to display other
virtues, to display a constant cheerfulness under all skies, no
matter how dark or lowering. To return in thought to the
opening words of this chapter—whatever else I cannot do,
there is never a time or a place when and where I cannot put
on a good courage if only I will. Jesus tells me that even if I
take up a cross and bear it as He did, my hope need not be
confounded. Therefore, by His example, I resolve that hope
shall be my badge and testimony when I have little else to say
and all my other armour is gone.

SIX

Moral Excellence

FOR want of a satisfactory definition, I have called the Christlike quality which I want to describe in this chapter 'moral excellence'. Perhaps I can best introduce it by a personal reminiscence. When I was very young I thought of Jesus as the one who could help me to be a better child of God, and I thought often, though superficially, of the difference between my life, in which there were many faults, and His life, in which there were none. I found no difficulty then in thinking of Jesus as morally perfect or, to use the Bible word, 'sinless'. My religious teachers encouraged me to imagine Jesus facing the same sort of moral problems and situations as I faced; but they told me that whereas I so often failed miserably, He always faced them successfully. At the end of each day, when I said my prayers, I asked forgiveness of the things I had wrongly done, and the other things I ought to have done but had neglected. I can remember many times, while on my knees at the bedside, the reflection passing through my mind that never at the end of a day in His earthly life would Jesus have had anything to regret. He would have done nothing wrong and left no good thing undone. That was my childlike idea of His perfect character; it was simple and it was satisfactory. Now it is neither. I am no logical positivist, but it does seem to me now that, strictly speaking, to say that Jesus was morally perfect, or that He was sinless, is to say something that is not significant. Therefore it is idle to claim that either of these statements is true.

Moral perfection or sinlessness may indeed be the sort of words we use to describe something about Jesus that God knows to be true, but for us they are words without specific reference and therefore without precise meaning. We cannot *know* them to be true. Let me illustrate. As a child I found

no difficulty in thinking that Jesus was perfect in knowledge
and in action, but now that I have attained to some sort of
intellectual maturity I realize that to ascribe to Jesus a perfect
acquaintance with the second law of thermodynamics, for
instance, or a knowledge of the geographical position of every
South Sea island, is absurd. There are still ardent funda-
mentalists who become greatly indignant when I say in Hyde
Park that Jesus thought that the earth was flat, but to think
that He carried in His mind all the accumulated knowledge
that has come to us down the years will make a monstrosity of
that mind. What is more serious—if Jesus knew the medical
answer to cancer, for instance, which as yet eludes us, and kept
silent about it, His intellectual perfection is being maintained
at the expense of His moral goodness; for one who knew how
to cure that fell disease but kept that knowledge to Himself
stands condemned at the bar of ordinary neighbourliness.

Paul came to grips with this problem and frankly recognized
that the human Jesus was God 'self-emptied' of many of His
eternal powers. Yet it is not, I contend, sufficient to say that
Jesus was imperfect in the realm of practical knowledge alone.
That imperfection must have been reflected in imperfect
judgements. Disappointment in the lack of faith demonstrated by His disciples (and represented by His question that
began 'How is it?') is the mark of an imperfect understanding
of the characters of those disciples. If He had known them
better He would have been less perturbed at their faithlessness;
if he had known them perfectly He would not have been disappointed at all. The imperfection of His knowledge resulted
in an imperfection in His judgement. Again, if we completely
agree that Jesus had an intrinsically human body, and I sometimes wonder how those who believe implicitly in the Virgin
Birth of our Lord can maintain this contention, then once
again 'perfection' appears to me an impossible word to use
with any clear meaning. Nothing is more certain than that the
body exercises a powerful influence upon our disposition, our
words, our mental and moral reactions—in short, upon our
personality itself.

What, for instance, does perfection mean when we think of

the normal physical ailments which Jesus, as a boy, under-
went; when we think of Him mellowed by wine, nervously
exhausted by overwork, on edge with hunger, or depressed
with pain and sickness? If such thoughts offend, then face
the alternative of a Jesus who was impervious to such mental
and moral influences, and you are left with an inconceivable
and preposterous theory. What you certainly are not left with
is anything recognizable as a man.

The word 'sinless' (in its narrower sense) when applied to
Jesus seems equally unsatisfactory. To think of Jesus as a
sinless boy of ten, say, I find simply impossible. Was He not
mischievous, untidy, forgetful, egotistic, boastful? Once
again, when we use a word like 'sinless' to describe a growing
lad we are simply using a word which has no real significance.
At the risk of offence, I would press the reader to face this
matter with vigorous care. It is easy to preach and proclaim
Jesus as a perfect man, and by that ascription to infer that His
life was ethically immaculate. Yet if 'sinlessness' is meant to
convey the idea that Jesus met every single temptation with
an immaculate moral response, or if it means the complete
absence of any sense of moral imperfection, then quite frankly
I can have no conception of what that means. Moreover, to
try to imagine any twenty-four hours in the life of Jesus as a
young man, and within that period to arrive at a mental picture
of our Lord behaving impeccably down to the smallest detail
of conversation, becomes the more impossible as it is undertaken the more seriously. So intimately are the limitations
which belong to human nature associated with the human will,
that I find a rigid doctrine of sinlessness, when applied to
Jesus, a string of empty words.

Yet, paradoxically, I want to preserve the idea which has
prompted the theologians to describe Jesus as sinless, because
deep down in me I have the conviction that He is not just
better morally than I am, but that within His human framework He achieved the topmost peak of moral quality. I
remember I once received 'excellent' for an essay I wrote, and
alongside it the mark '10 out of 10'. I am satisfied that under
strict examination, that essay would not have been found to

be perfect either in syntax or in construction, and I am sure that the teacher who marked it did not intend to convey the impression that at long last a scholar in his class had written the essay to end all essays—the archetypal essay. But I do remember what he was generous enough to say about it; 'Soper,' said he, 'your essay is chock full of good things.' May I suggest that when we are thinking of Jesus, it is as realistic to think of the excellence of His character as it is unrealistic to think of His sinlessness—at least for ordinary people like ourselves who are not schooled in scholastic or other philosophical ideas. Because this book makes no pretence to a comprehensive statement on the person of Christ, I will invite the reader again to see what I am so imperfectly trying to say, by standing at the foot of the Cross and looking at the dying Master.

We are so familiar, at least superficially, with the sombre episodes crowded into those few hours, that some of the extraordinary elements in them remain disregarded. Jesus, for instance, gave no suggestion whatsoever that He was endeavouring to maintain on the Cross any record of sinlessness —it was some eternal good that He sought to fulfil. And He did gloriously 'fulfil all righteousness', so that near the end of those three hours He cried out in triumph: 'It is finished.' The moral emphasis was on the positive good that He had to do rather than any sin He had to avoid. So great was the expulsive power of His love, that sin, as the falling short of that love, could win no foothold in His spirit. He was filled to the brim with goodness, and He expressed in His dying the truth of His own words in the Sermon on the Mount: 'Resist not evil, but overcome evil with good.'

Of all men, Jesus was least preoccupied with sin; He recognized it for what it was, perceived and practised its antidote, and thereafter was free to ignore it. Our obsession with it is surely the mark of our failure to know Christ. The Church has felt compelled to preach its Lord as technically sinless precisely because it has not been ready to proclaim His moral excellence. The same is true of the individual Christian who endeavours to compensate for a life only a quarter full of positive goodness by seeking after the negative merit of avoiding sins. Jesus warns me that an over-solicitous care to keep clear of sin is probably due to a laziness and unreadiness to take up the cross. I look at Him and I am amazed at the overflowing fountain of His goodness—never ceasing, never abating—the indefatigable love for His fellow men, and the unflagging zeal with which He bought up every precious moment that He might fill it with love, and love for unworthy fellows such as ourselves. In this vision, what have I to do with academic discussions about academic sinlessness? My business is not with Christian perfection as the entire absence of any roots of sin; it is with perfect love as the excellence of the God-filled life. Jesus is my great example. He it is who inspires me to pray:

> *Fill every part of me with praise;*
> *Let all my being speak*
> *Of Thee and of Thy love, O Lord,*
> *Poor though I be and weak.*

There is another aspect of this moral excellence of Jesus which greatly moves me. I call it to mind as I think of Him on the Cross. It is His naturalness. Once again words are the bugbear, but I will try to use them significantly. One of the characteristics of Church people today, and I daresay of all the yesterdays as well, is a kind of unnatural tension. How often does the Christian appear to the man in the street to be a kind of moral alien, or, rather, one who assumes an alien role. They tell me on Tower Hill that their quarrel with us is that we are a bit queer. We, according to them, make people feel uncomfortable, not so much because we are so good, but because we are so peculiar. The good red blood seems to have been thinned out in our arteries, and in the interests of our immortal souls we have filled ourselves with sawdust. 'If only you'd be yourselves', they complain, 'instead of putting on an act.'

Now, this is all exaggerated, as usual, but it is not without substance. Piety does dehydrate some earnest souls. Worse

E

still, it tends to induce a glare in the eyes and a humourless zeal which are thought to be valid evidences of sanctity. That all this is the tell-tale flush of unnaturalness is as plain as a pikestaff, and in order to validate this statement there is no need to remind ourselves of the way in which revivalism has so often been marked by fierce asceticism eked out with spasms of sexual dissipation. In its milder forms it can be seen at almost any Sunday-school picnic or Church ramble, where decorum and horseplay jostle for pre-eminence. When the true naturalness of the good life is lost, then the spasms of moral asceticism and moral licence take its place. For me Tolstoi is the classic example of this truth, and a comparison between this undoubtedly good and great man and his Lord throws a vivid light upon this whole question. At one time Tolstoi was striving with heroic ardour to extirpate the vices within him; at another time he seemed abandoned to excesses and to complete moral irresponsibility, only to turn back afterwards in loathing of his sins. In neither condition did he strike his contemporaries, let alone his wife, as completely natural, though some of his friends liked him the better when he was the less hagridden with sanctification.

With Jesus all is different. He seemed almost careless of what others thought about Him. He felt not the slightest need, as far as we can judge, to make a demonstration of His goodness, and seems to have impressed friends and enemies alike with his unaffected beauty of character. Looking at Him I want to pray again and again:

> *Take from our souls the strain and stress,*
> *And let our ordered lives confess*
> *The beauty of Thy peace.*

It is perhaps an abrupt jump from that hymn to a popular musical play, in which there is a song about 'Doing what comes naturally'. Yet that does describe the moral excellence of our Lord. I am sure that to His disciples the goodness of Jesus was the doing of what came naturally to Him, but they were not such simpletons as to think that the deceptive ease with which Jesus practised the love of God was a virtue 'un-exercised and unbreathed'. What the Cross did bring home to their spirits was that the goodness of Jesus was that natural state of man which sin had defaced, and which their suffering Master was recovering for them.

SEVEN

Faith

IT has always struck me, when thinking about the person of Christ, that if we are to talk about His faith we must above all be careful to preserve a belief in His humanity. Undue zeal in the proclamation of His divinity, let alone His Deity, cannot, as I see it, avoid the destruction of any intelligible meaning for the word 'faith' when applied to Jesus. The Fathers of the Church, who never failed to recognize the problems that their credal statements involved, though they were not necessarily able to answer those problems, saw this dilemma quite clearly. If Jesus lived in a state of unbroken intimacy with His father, if there was no cloud, however small, that hid the Father's face, if Jesus was at one with God in every respect and at all times, then to talk of His faith in God is non-significant. Again, if Jesus shared the perfect knowledge of God about the world, the flesh, and the devil, then to talk of His faith in His disciples or His Kingdom is equally meaningless. He already possessed the substance of things hoped for. He had the irrefragible evidence of things not seen. Thus the Church Fathers saw that to press His claims to be the Son of God too rigorously would be to undermine the reality of many of the human experiences recorded of His ministry and of His Passion. He hoped great things from his disciples; He was astonished at the unbelieving resistance of the religious leaders; He prayed for help to the Father in the garden; He struggled to keep His faith; He declared with His last words from the Tree His affirmation of trust in God. All these aspects of His life and work would have nothing more than the characteristics of play-acting if in fact there had been no gulf of doubt or consciousness of nescience that stretched between His spirit and God's, like that which yawns between ours and God's. One of the more mechanical attempts to resolve this difficulty has been to divide the life and experiences of our Lord into two, and to say that there were some periods when He enjoyed the perfect knowledge that only God possesses, because He was God, and others when He suffered the limitations of a man's nature, because He was man. Thus, it is argued, the two natures took turns within the same body, and when He was acting as the Son of Man He expressed the faith for which He had no need when He was acting as the Son of God.

Psychologically such a theory is an intellectual shambles and only survives where genuine thinking about these issues is ignored. To the other orthodox and historic attempt to face this problem by calling up Paul's idea that the Son of God 'emptied Himself of all but love' I have already referred briefly. Suffice it to say here that the assertion that the Jesus who is eternally with the Father consciously divested Himself of certain attributes, so that He might at a precise moment in time became man, becomes more difficult to subsume under any clear intellectual concept the more closely it is examined. I feel, for instance, that if Jesus carried in His human consciousness the remembrance of this self-conscious emptying of His Divine powers and status, then once again to talk of His faith is to talk of something radically different from the sort of faith to which we may aspire. It is only surely possible to speak of the faith of Jesus if, as a man, He was not only emptied of those Divine attributes, but unaware that He had indeed possessed them.

You may, gentle reader, think all this matters little. The justification I claim for raising these matters at all is that I think it is of absolute importance that, when we ponder the characteristics of Jesus, we should be able to start with the confidence that our Lord's human nature was substantially the same as ours. For me it is infinitely precious that I can look upon Jesus as my ideal as well as my Saviour, the Master who calls me to follow Him as well as the Lord who claims my worship. Therefore, in considering His faith, I shall be concerned to start with Jesus as a man limited by the same frontiers of the mind as those which surround me, and invested with none of those supra-human qualities which, seeing that He dwells no longer in the flesh, He now possesses. Let me begin there without any sense of irreverence. Let me come to Him as the disciples did; let me attend to Him simply and attentively as man to man, believing that if I can be sure of His humanity, His divinity will speak through that humanity.

In beginning this pilgrimage, the first thing that impresses me about the faith of Jesus is that in fact it is compounded of the same stuff of which my own is made. Though its quality and breadth are marvellous, whereas my faith is weak and small, I notice the same elements in His faith that I find in my own, or that I fain would find in my own. To begin with, I recognize the element of struggle. The faith of Jesus was not an effortless possession. There is a certain serenity about it, a royal assurance that pervades it, but His frequent need for quietness and prayer show this faith to be an achievement rather than a gift, an achievement moreover which needed constant protection and buttressing.

I am glad of this, for throughout my ministry I have been plagued by those who apparently find religious faith as easy to accept as the sight of their eyes, and as obvious as the toes on their feet. Their aptitude for, and easy digestion of, all sorts of dogmas which I cannot even get my teeth into is both astonishing and, I confess, irritating. Evangelists who swallow the Bible whole, ecclesiastics who swallow the Church whole, prelates who swallow righteousness whole—are they really exponents of faith, or are they the victims of credulity? To me it is incredible that intelligent people should embrace with a sort of exotic pleasure the most extraordinary nonsense about spiritual matters while maintaining the most rigorous mental vigilance in matters temporal. I can think of brilliant scientists (particularly medical men) who seem able to combine an almost cynically critical attitude to the human body with what seems to me a lunatic credence in the physical return of our Lord.

For me, faith in God is hard to come by and harder to keep. A fairly extensive acquaintance with the more modern forms of dialectical materialism has not aggravated this condition, but it has pin-pointed it. I do not know whether I am typical of men of my own age and intellectual environment, but the arguments *against* a belief in Theism are to me almost as persuasive as those *for* it. Purely from the static and academic standpoint I should be compelled in honesty to describe myself as an agnostic, because the evidence that comes to me from the various fields of human experience does not, in my judgement, add up to any coherent pattern.

What changes a would-be agnosticism into a vibrant faith is both the practical need for, and the actual process of, faith. The very effort to believe is in itself a creative activity; the very search for faith is its own reward. In a most imperfect fashion I have proved this to be true beyond doubting. When I first began to speak out of doors, and particularly when I began to try to answer the heckler, I noticed time and again a feeling of certitude in the heat of the argument, that I knew at no other time. Part of this, I am now sure was not genuine faith, but the strong desire to win the day by putting an intellectual case for Christianity, which I did not necessarily believe at all. But was it nothing more than an intellectual game played for the satisfaction of winning? No! I found as a matter of fact, that the effort and struggle of the open-air meeting itself produced a state of faith which was unique. To put it very simply, I enjoyed a confident certainty on Tower Hill and in Hyde Park which I experienced at no other time.

This experience threw a new and significant light on the advice which Peter Böhler is reported to have given to John Wesley: 'Preach faith until you get it.' Better still, it underscored the profound insight of our Lord's own words: 'Seek and ye shall find; ask and ye shall receive; knock and it shall be opened unto you.' I now see how precious is the need to struggle after a faith, how childish it is to complain that belief in God is not easy. Credence without effort is valueless for such credence is not born in faith at all, but in the uncriticized condition of suggestibility.

The Gospel writers make no attempt to conceal the strong

element of effort that accompanied our Lord's faith. This
struggle is critically stressed in the prayer in the Garden and
in the cry of desolation on the Cross. Whether that cry was or
was not a temporary setback in that otherwise victorious
struggle, whether it was or was not the depicting of that
struggle in terms of the whole Psalm of which 'My God, why
hast Thou forsaken me?' are the opening words, the Gospels
are at pains to show that the price of faith for Jesus Himself
was 'sweat like great drops of blood'. I thank God that the
Master who calls me to believe is not only the example of the
end of that process, but also the example of the way which
leads to that end.

Closely linked with this aspect of faith is the wider and
perhaps more familiar idea which, strangely enough, was
dramatically restated by none other than Karl Marx. Marx
announced, with all the authority of an Old Testament
prophet, that 'truth is only possible in a unity of thought and
action'. Like so many other Marxist dicta, it was neither
original nor revolutionary. It was, on the other hand, a most
valuable recovery, for the time in which he lived, of a religious precept common to both the great religious traditions—
those that arose in the east under the various forms of Hindu-
ism and those that developed in the west in the various
expressions of Christo-Judaistic cultures. There is no such
thing as purely academic faith. As an experience it is never
found in the purely intellectual processes. Because it belongs
to the living world of human beings it is always fallacious to
isolate it from the flux of human personality. Faith always
contains an admixture of practical activity. Although it is
often convenient to make distinctions between 'thought, feeling,
and conation (wilfulness)', the familiar trilogy which we use to
express the set-up of a human personality, we can be sure that
these three are never separable; they are only distinguishable,
or present in varying proportions. In any belief, there is not
only a predominantly intellectual characteristic, but there is
also an element of feeling, and, most important for the present
discussion, there is always the activity of the will. Strictly
speaking, faith only exists in the form of acts of faith. All faith

by its very nature is dynamic; it is the 'saving' faith, the 'living' faith of John Wesley's sermons, the active confiding which is perhaps best described as *trust*.

Let me try to put this in the plainest of ways. When I pray that my faith may be stronger, and that I may have an inward assurance of the great claims of the Christian religion, I must pray first of all, not for a serene mind, but for a faithful will. I cannot have faith by itself first, and then express that faith in Christian discipleship afterwards. Like my Master, my faith and my discipleship must go together. At one time it will be the evidence of that faith that will come more strongly to my mind, at another it will be the practical demands of vesting my life in God that will present themselves more forcibly to my will, but at all times it is my life which I must offer to God in a supreme adventure. I know that faith is so often described in Christian literature, as in the New Testament, as a gift. 'By grace are ye saved through faith, and that not of yourselves, it is the gift of God', but the gift is only vouchsafed to those who are already acting as if they possess it. True, the gift is not of ourselves, but ours is the hand which must be stretched out in trust to receive it.

I should like to be of particular help, in what I write, to those who, like myself, have a lively, if not particularly profound, awareness of the intellectual problems that hedge a belief in the God and Father of our Lord Jesus Christ. Jesus repeatedly warned His disciples to begin their thinking about God and the Gospel by using the mental apparatus with which they were naturally endowed. He said it much more simply and trenchantly: 'He that hath ears to hear, let him hear.' To me, these words constitute the Magna Charta of Christian thinking. The rights of my mind will never be abrogated by the claims that God makes upon me. I shall not be pressed to believe that which by the canons of ordinary common sense is absurd or self-contradictory. I can open my ears with confidence to listen to all that comes to me from the world which God asks me to believe is His. Nothing that comes to me from any part of that realm will make such a belief fundamentally unreasonable. Whatever I hear will leave room for faith, but what I hear will not create faith, it will only provide the raw material for that faith.

The companion words of Jesus to 'He that hath ears to hear, let him hear' are 'Come unto me and learn of me'. I come with a mind not made up, but with all the elements necessary for that making up. I must make up my mind. I must take the various thoughts and facts, the evidence for and against a Christian faith, and I must do something with them—just as I am—not waiting for either a heart that is pure or a mind that is free from doubt. I must set out upon the road that leads to God.

The one necessity for that journey is that the road must be open—that it must not be a blind alley or blocked by insurmountable obstructions. But that necessity has already been attended to; the road is clear, and it will never be blocked. I am certain of this truth, because not even Calvary was able to shut this road for Jesus. Even in the throes of this unique test, Jesus was able to make His unfaltering way along it. And now and always He keeps it open for me and for all doubting sinners. If I choose to trust in God, nothing finally can forbid me. My mind will not tell me that such a venture of faith is intellectually absurd; my will can still plant my feet firmly in the footmarks of my Lord. I can say with Paul: 'I am persuaded that neither death nor life, nor angels, nor principalities, nor powers, nor things present, nor things to come, nor height, nor depth, nor any other creature, shall be able to separate us from the love of God, which is in Christ Jesus our Lord' (Romans 8[38-9]).

EIGHT

Love

IN the lovely hymn attributed to Bernard of Clairvaux—

> *Jesu, the very thought of Thee*
> *With sweetness fills my breast—*

there is a line which once perplexed me for long enough, although I have not come across any general concern about it. Bernard's words are translated:

> *The love of Jesus, what it is*
> *None but His loved ones know.*

The plain meaning of this, at least to me, is that only those who are loved by Jesus can understand what His love is like. But we surely believe that Jesus' love pours out 'immense, unfathomed, unconfined' upon us all? Jesus does not select those today to whom He manifests His love; His is an 'undistinguishing regard' that embraces us all. It is tragically true, moreover, that most of those to whom the love of Jesus is offered are entirely unaware of the wonderful gift they ignore. Unfortunately, to be beloved by Jesus does not carry with it the bestowal of understanding, let alone of reciprocation. Most of His loved ones have little or no idea of what the love of Jesus means. This for me was quite a sizeable problem; and how delighted I was to find that the translation by Edward Caswell of this hymn was inaccurate. The original means:

> *The love of Jesus what it is*
> *None but His lovers know*

The translator felt that the word 'lovers' had a somewhat erotic association and preferred the innocuous 'loved-ones' but only the original words have real significance—and how true they are. To know the love of Jesus is impossible if

we merely contemplate that love; it comes alive to us only
when we seek to respond to it by loving Him as ardently as
we can, in the way shown to us in His life and teaching and
finally upon the Cross. For that reason it is impossible to
treat the love of Jesus in an academic fashion. There are
certain broad aspects of it which I shall try to describe,
but at heart this love is a 'lovers' secret'. In fact, even
those general characteristics of His love, those elements in it
which make it such a different thing from what we so often call
love, defeat the attempt of the best words we know to describe
them. I hope that I can say something to make this truth
plainer as I endeavour to write of the love of Jesus as it shines
from the Cross. But, first, there is another difficulty in describing our Lord's love. It is that, like other aspects of His
Person, we have taken the word itself so easily and so often
upon our lips that we assume that we know what it means,
and that it is sufficient for our devotions, as well as our evangelism, to assert that He loved us and that He gave himself
for us.

To me as a boy the statement that 'God loves us because He
gives us Jesus' was offered in many sermons as a convincing
and sufficient description of the love of God. It had in fact
the opposite effect. I did not feel that any father had a right to
give his son over to death even for the highest purposes. It
seemed to me to reflect the action of an Oriental despot rather
than of a loving father. With great patience ministers ex-
plained to me the inner meaning of John 3¹⁶: 'For God so
loved the world, that he gave his only begotten Son, that
whosoever believeth in him should not perish, but have ever-
lasting life'; and I daresay they were right. The point I am
stressing is that the text as it stands is not self-explanatory,
though for those who bring to it insights from elsewhere it
will, of course, have great devotional value. As a statement of
the love of God it begs the question. Similarly, to say that
Jesus' love consists in His self-giving is profoundly true, but
it has become a cliché instead of an exposition. As a friend of
mine in Warsaw said to me: 'Our minds are so full of slogans
that finally we do not think at all.'

This is not only the menace that confronts the one who thinks about political truth; it is the equally dangerous stumbling block to the would-be seeker after spiritual truth. I would cordially invite my friends in M.R.A., for instance, to believe that, inasmuch as they have used slogans to describe love and purity and honesty, they have ceased to make any real effort to understand these tremendous words. This is the underlying truth in the copy-book axiom that words are used to conceal thought. Words become so often the mess of pottage for which we sell our intellectual birthright. I know men on Tower Hill whose brows are puckered until they can find a simplification of words which gives to them an appearance of veracity. Never mind how complicated the problem and how metaphysical the issue, such men have conditioned themselves to accept this pattern of words as satisfying and final. The moment they hear the familiar phrase, their brows become clear, their problems are over. What they entirely fail to realize is that they have achieved contentment by closing their minds, not by using them. This is always a disastrous method, and never so devastating as when we allow it to govern our attitude to the greatest thing in this world—love.

In thinking, then, of the love of Jesus, let me start out at a different place altogether. If God is love, and Jesus is God incarnate, then the life and death of Jesus are expositions of that Divine love; and to see clearly that life, and especially that death, is to see love clearly. This is to me so vitally important that I should like to repeat what I have just said in another form. The love of Jesus is something that happens—its essence is in action rather than in feeling. I do not know whether Jesus liked, for instance, either Judas or the Pharisees. If 'to like' means 'to feel a natural sense of personal attraction', then I feel that there must have been many people who can have produced no such feelings in our Lord. Our capacity to like people would appear to me to be very severely limited. This capacity depends upon, and is conditioned by, so many factors which are not ours to create or control. If we fall *in love* we must assuredly fall *into our likes and dislikes*. There is nothing either praiseworthy or blameworthy in these primitive reactions, and in so far as they do not come within the realm of the will, I cannot believe that there can be any divine law requiring us to like everybody. Having established this proposition, I hope upon a reasonable foundation, I would add my gratitude for it. I find it quite impossible to like some people I know—even some who are models of rectitude.

Loving is radically different from liking. It is probable that Jesus liked many of the publicans and sinners who were found in His company, as much as He disliked many of the religious leaders of His day. I should think that there is evidence of a strong bond of affection (strong liking) between Jesus and John as there is evidence of antipathy (strong disliking) on the part of Jesus toward Herod. The Love of Jesus, on the other hand, was the living response of the whole personality to other personalities whether He liked them or not. Nothing is clearer from the passion narrative, especially of John, than this. We are not told at length how warmly Jesus felt. His love was goodwill on fire; the warmth was in the fire of His ceaseless efforts to do men good. Studdert Kennedy, with his usual perceptiveness, captures this sense of love by the simple repetition: 'To give, and give, and give again as God hath given thee.' That untiring outpouring of Himself in kindly deeds, creative words, selfless service, was not the effect of His love. It was the thing itself. Love is the doing of good.

I think of a particular piece of social work in connexion with the Mission where I work. In an old and transformed nineteenth-century casual ward we seek to care for more than a hundred destitute people—the poor relations of the 'down-and-outs'. Technically, they are entitled to the sort of help that the Welfare State offers in its various institutions. Practically, because of mental peculiarities or personal habits, these most unfortunate people, both men and women, are unacceptable in any of these State-provided hostels. Putting it bleakly, if they were housed in these institutions the other inmates would raise bitter and continuous complaint and would create an intolerable situation. The hostel represents the continuing need for someone to care for the one in a community which cares for the ninety-and-nine. When talking about this piece of rescue work, I come across those who say how wonderful it must be to have a hand in such a romantic service, how lovely it must be to tend these poor old people, and how moving to hear their whispered thanks and to see their wrinkled faces break into gratitude. I wish it were like this, but it is not. Most of the people cared for in the Hungerford Hostel are not lovely or grateful, but warped and grudging and unpleasant. The blame may well rest not on them but on the society which has laid almost insupportable burdens upon them. The fact however remains that most of these people who are cared for in this place of Christian service are mentally warped, personally unattractive, and often verminous and neurotic. To like such caricatures of what God intended men and women to be is well-nigh impossible. Yet they can be, and are loved, and that love is a matter of 'putting up with them', of cleansing them of their vermin, of attending to their unpleasant demands, in short, of serving them despite the aesthetic distaste which is unavoidable. Thus, the wardens and voluntary workers at the Hungerford Hostel love those whom it is impossible to like, and so in their humble way they follow in the steps of their Lord.

This total activity of the personality in the service of others is the love that shines from the Cross. Jesus was—to use the somewhat ugly but significant phrase that, I imagine, started its life across the Atlantic Ocean—utterly 'expendable'. There was no nice calculation of the moral excellence of those upon whom this love was showered. 'God commendeth His love toward us, that while we were yet sinners Christ died for us' is a tremendous assertion, made, I think, all too often with only one aspect of that truth in our mind. Sinners are not only morally degraded; they become of less and less worth, until they appear to be morally worthless. Heine is reported to have said: 'I, too, would have been prepared to die for men had I not shrewdly suspected that they were not worth it.' I tend to shy away from this cynical remark with wholehearted disapproval, but it haunts me and rebukes me. It is well-nigh impossible for me to separate the act of love from the assumed worth of the recipient of that love. Yet the great act of love upon the Cross is unmistakable evidence that for Jesus no such calculation made the slightest difference. It was not for Him to weigh the gifts of His love against the moral worth of His tormentors and of His frightened disciples. The mark of eternal value, even of the most brutal soldier taking part in the dreadful torture of nailing the hands of Jesus to the wood, had been imprinted by God, and therefore in simple faith Jesus loved that soldier.

This love which is rooted in the will rather than the feelings has a simplifying and clarifying effect upon my own thinking, and can be, I am sure, of great comfort and encouragement to many who find the gospel of love bewildering. As in so many other areas of the moral life, our own responsibilities are limited by the words: 'God who knoweth our frailties and remembereth that we are dust.' There have been times when I have chastened myself because I have felt little or no zest for the life of Christian love. Was I not a hypocrite to continue the preaching of a way of life for which there seemed so little inward confirmation? How could I proclaim the way of love while I was filled with doubts and empty of assurance? I know that such experiences as these are by no means rare even among the noblest of my ministerial colleagues. I know now that if I am not a hypocrite on other grounds I need fear no indictment here. What God requires of me is that which He perfectly received from Jesus—the performance of goodwill, the persistent intention to seek the good of others. With this He is content, and I must be content to await the refreshing showers of assurance and personal security which finally He will not withhold. How often I remember in this regard the very wise words of Baron von Hugel: 'I kiss my child not first because I love him, but that I may love him.'

Again, there have also been times when I have been flung almost into cynicism because of the apparent ineffectiveness of love as a transforming power in this wicked world. I have clamoured for success, as I suppose from time to time we all do—not necessarily of a personal kind, but success for the Christian faith—and so often it has not been forthcoming in anything like the dimensions that I wanted to see.

One of the responsibilities of the West London Mission is the care of 'delinquent girls'. Some are prostitutes, some are near prostitutes, some are in need of care and protection if they are to come through to decent womanhood; all are cared for magnificently by wise and Christian wardens. All are surrounded by understanding and love, and over the years much wisdom has been steadily acquired as to the best way of utilizing the six months during which these girls reside at the Katherine Price Hughes Hostel. What proportion of them become converted to Christianity and join the Methodist, or any other, Church? A very small proportion indeed. What proportion of them seek a complete moral recovery and set out upon a new and better road?—ten per cent at most. Are there not many who remain obdurate and impervious to all the love showered upon them?—yes there are. Then isn't it all a waste of time and effort? Of course not, for even if only one out of hundreds were set on her feet and turned to the light the effort would be more than worthwhile. But beside such a consideration, there is another, the truth of which has come to me the more slowly. The responsibility of the Christian is to provide the 'service of love' to these unfortunate girls. The moment we begin to calculate the effectiveness of that service we are out of our depth and floundering in an uncharted sea. Love does not cease to be love when its effects are inconclusive by our standards of judgement. Love does not cease to be love when only God can see its fruit. I have learnt by looking at Jesus crucified to be content to practise that love and not to demand visible and immediate proof that it works, and I am beginning to find that such love is its own reward.

Nevertheless, it would be an unrealistic contraction of the meaning of love to attach it solely to the wilful performance of good acts. Alongside this practical seeking of the well-being of others is another element, which, I suggest, can best be described as tenderness. Now, tenderness is another word with a deceptively simple appearance to the unwary mind. If suddenly confronted with the word, would not most of us associate it with an activity? Should we not see it as one way of expressing the truth of the foregoing paragraphs of this

F

chapter? Yet such is not the root idea of tenderness. A tender heart is like a tender finger, and the outstanding characteristic of a tender finger is that it can easily be hurt, it is susceptible to pain. The characteristic nature of tenderness is vulnerability—the capacity to be hurt. There is also, of course, a more positive meaning which accompanies it, namely a capacity to respond to other impacts besides those which occasion pain, for example, responsiveness to joy and pleasure in our fellow creatures. Love is a condition of sensitivity to other people. It is the direct opposite of indifference, and is the moral core of neighbourliness.

In one sense, and within certain narrow limits, all of us participate in, and express, this kind of love. I know that I love my little daughter, because her laughter rejoices my heart and her pain stabs me. Similarly, the great marital promise, 'they shall become one flesh', glows with a new significance as I think of the love I bear my wife. The bruise that afflicts her body is a hurt to mine. I feel it with an acuteness which, except in the strictest material sense, could not be keener if it were in fact my flesh which was receiving the pain and not hers. This is more than a comradeship of suffering, it is a sort of 'identification' (to use one of the psychological terms that is popular in this context). To experience this tender identification is one of the sublime realities of human life, perhaps the most sublime.

But, however charmed the circle of our human love, how small is that circle. If, as I write these words, a message were brought to me that one of my children had been suddenly stricken with pain, that message would cut into me like a knife. But if a message were here and now brought to me in this room telling me of the sudden striking of millions of God's children with pain, would such a message cut me like a knife? It would not—it does not—for I am intellectually aware of this melancholy fact every day of my life. How miserably restricted is the circle within which I feel tenderness toward others. Those who are wise in matters of human personality tell us that it would be intolerable if our feelings were continually lacerated by the effects of such tenderness, and that a constant emotion of tenderness would be insupportable. This may be so. Being the sort of person that I am, I can well believe that I am not morally staunch enough to bear such a weight of sympathetic feeling, but this again really begs the question. Maybe the only means by which I could grow more tender would be by exposing myself to greater emotional stresses as the area of my sympathy became enlarged. The point at the moment is that I ought to be ashamed that my love is so small and my indifference so widespread.

Looking at Jesus dying on the Cross I see this tenderness *in excelsis*. Quotations and allusions leap to the mind, and I will leave the reader to summon up such words from the Bible or the Prayer Book or the Hymn-book as seem most apposite to him. I think of the words of Isaiah: 'He bore our griefs and carried our sorrows, he was wounded for our transgressions.' I remember the repeated emphasis in hymn after hymn, that He feels 'what every member bears'.

All combine to testify to that supreme love which makes the lover tender to all, so that there is no sorrow so light or so remote but that He feels that sorrow to be His own. Moreover there is joy over the most insignificant sinner that repents. Here is the full stature of manhood and the true image of the Father's love. Herein can I believe and say He loved me, He suffered for me, He gave himself for me. He identified himself with my life, its sorrows and its joys; He has drawn me with the cords of love, and thus He has bound me to Him.

There is infinitely more to be said about the love of Jesus, and though inadequate, it will not, I think, be impertinent to finish this chapter with another comment on this particular quality of tenderness, or, more accurately, upon the final effect of this quality.

We know that half our troubles, personal and social, would disappear, and that the other half would be transformed, if we possessed the gift of putting ourselves in the other man's place. All the same it is exasperating merely to be exhorted to do so. That is what I find so unsatisfying in the otherwise wise words of men like Bertrand Russell, when they tell us that we should practise tolerance by entering into the background of other

people's attitudes, or that we need a more creative understanding of the frailties and virtues of others. We know that
what they say is coercively reasonable, but we also feel that
such attitudes are beyond our personal reach. Understanding,
tolerance, sympathetic appreciation of the other side and the
other person, are not qualities that we can come by just as an
intellectual process, and then, as the simple translation of that
thought, put into action. At the foot of the Cross I am taught
that these graces flow from a supreme grace, and are unattain-
able without that supreme grace. I am no longer surprised
that through the teaching of Jesus, love is given the pre-
cminence over all other moral qualities. It is the supreme
grace because it is the dayspring of goodness. Love conquers
all, because it is the key that finally opens every door; to vary
the image, love is the light that illuminates the whole house of
our being, for it is the master switch which, when turned,
makes alive every other switch in every single room.

I hear Jesus say to me, as long ago He said to Peter: 'Do
you love me?'—and like Peter I only appreciate part of the
meaning of that question. Therefore, I answer all too easily:
'Yes, I love you.' Be a true minister and pastor of my flock,
says Jesus, and with those words I imagine that the conversation is properly concluded. But He asks the same question
again and again, until I am compelled to see that there is some
mysterious and profound connexion between loving Him and
doing His work. The love that can bring me close to Him is
the source of grace and tenderness, without which I cannot
really care for the flock as a true shepherd. My self-sufficiency,
like that of Peter, is gone. Everything depends on Him, my
hope and my love are in Him. I say with Peter: 'Master, Thou
knowest all things.'

Thus, contemplating the character of Jesus as revealed at
Calvary, and looking upon His love, I pass beyond the stage
of seeking a clearer understanding of His superb virtues.
Having begun there, I am irresistibly led to the point where I
need Him to expound these virtues, and better still to impart
them. He says learn of me, but thereafter He says, 'Come unto
me and I will give you'—give you those qualities which you

have learnt from me and begin now to desire. Throughout these chapters hitherto, the assumption has been made that by coming to Jesus we can indeed possess the single-mindedness, humility, courage, and love, that are the glory of His life and passion. It should be remembered that in the eyes of even sympathetic outsiders, this claim appears to be stupendous; to the rest it appears nothing better than preposterous. What, if anything, is the 'end product' of looking at the Cross? Does virtue flow like the blood from His wounds. William Cowper sang:

> There is a fountain filled with blood
>   Drawn from Immanuel's veins;
> And sinners, plunged beneath that flood,
>   Lose all their guilty stains.

If this amazing claim is true, then the open secret of the universe is ours at the foot of the Cross. If it is not, our human history, and especially that episode in it which took place 1,900 years ago without a city wall, is nothing better than a 'tale told by an idiot, full of sound and fury, signifying nothing'.

NINE

Grace Abounding

HONEST and reasonable men in every age and from every part of the world have recognized the moral excellence of Jesus. Even those who have claimed to have discovered lacunae in his character, or think that they have detected faults in His earthly behaviour, have yet agreed that in the matter of goodness Jesus is a giant. He towers above the rest of us. If this assertion needs further evidence of truth let me call to witness the best men who have lived since Jesus, and remind the reader that most of them have acclaimed Jesus as their moral superior, and many have been happy to call themselves His disciples and to acknowledge the grandeur of His ethical achievement.

All the same, to reflect on this matter may bring little comfort with it. Facing, as we do, complex and acute moral problems upon which depend the welfare of the whole world as well as our own inner peace, the unique moral goodness of Jesus may well make us feel hopeless, if not cynical. If He stands alone, and if His goodness is alone sufficient to meet the hazards and perils of this mortal existence of ours, then what hope have we lesser mortals? Is not our complete failure inevitable? If, since He flashed across the human screen, there has been no other like Him, and if those least unlike Him have insisted on the gulf that yet separates their ethical achievements from His, what right have we to talk of Christianity as good news? To put the issue immediately and personally, is there any point in thinking upon the goodness of Jesus, as we have been doing in these pages, if we are but watchers of a splendid, remote and inaccessible Everest of moral attainment? Have we hitherto in these pages begged the all-important questions? The questions I want to answer in this chapter are: Can the goodness of Jesus be communicated to the life of the Christian Church? and, if so, What are the means of that communication?

The answer to the first of these questions has been given again and again by the Saints of the Church, as well as by its credal statements; it is Yes. Jesus has not only shown us the will of God; He has not only manifested the good life; but, through the Cross on which He died, man may be reconciled to God—brought back to God, so that God's righteousness may be re-implanted in his sinful but forgiven soul. Jesus is not only the example of goodness; He is also its mediator. The grace (which is the word by which we sum up all the goodness of Jesus) can flow from its Author into the life of the believer. It is supernatural grace, primarily because it is the perfect combination of all virtues, unsullied by selfishness, or pride, or any sin; and at the same time it is available grace, because it is offered to us by Jesus, who says: 'Come unto me and I will give you . . .'

We are not, therefore, condemned to watch from afar what we can never possess. We are partakers of Christ's goodness. We do not deserve it, and we cannot of ourselves achieve it, but, to quote again that glorious Pauline sentence: 'By grace are ye saved through faith; and that not of yourselves: it is the gift of God.' All Catholic and Apostolic Christianity is at one in declaring that 'Jesus saves', because He offers us a way of escape from the penalty of our misdoings. That escape is not, as careless evangelists have sometimes proclaimed, the saving of an inert and unconscious victim drowning helplessly in the surf. It is the invigorating of that victim with strength and purpose so that He can swim safely to the shore. It is our business as Christians to testify to the good news that those marvellous qualities of love and courage and humility which are, as it were, locked up in the personality of Jesus can be transmitted to sinners like you and me. Much of this sublime truth is beyond our logical understanding, but what we can and must say is this:

> *He died that we might be forgiven,*
> *He died to make us good,*
> *That we might go at last to Heaven,*
> *Saved by His precious blood.*

The practical value of considering the grace of our Lord
Jesus Christ lies in the fact that we are considering the grace
that may be ours too. 'Jesus comes with all His grace, comes
to save a fallen race . . .' by giving Himself to us whom He
calls His friends.

Thus the Cross of Jesus is both the proclamation of the love
of God and at the same time the instrument of our salvation.
We Christians believe that mercy and righteousness flow from
Jesus crucified into the lives of penitent sinners, so that finally
'We may go where He has gone . . .' and partake of that blessed
life which He lived and for ever lives.

Such is the claim of the Christian religion, and nothing less
than such a claim is worthy to be called Christian. Most
people on this planet, of course, do not believe it—some
because they are already committed to faiths which necessarily
exclude such a belief, and others because they cannot accept
a self-subsistent spiritual world at all. To neither of these
groups is this book particularly directed. There is a third
group. It is composed of people who might be ready to venture
themselves upon this great claim if they could be satisfied
about, or at least see, the relevance of, the means whereby, this
miracle happens. However, to pronounce this dogma is not
enough to convince them. They ask, quite reasonably, to be
told of the way or ways by which this grace is mediated. How
does it happen? Let me devote the remaining pages of this
book to some comments on the answer to this question.

The traditional Nonconformist answer, or at least the
common answer of Methodism during the last hundred years,
is that the spiritual phenomenon which mediates the Christlike
qualities to men and women such as we is in conversion.
Now whatever other elements there may be in conversion,
two are constant and imperative. Conversion is the act on the
part of the sinner in venturing his life upon the Saviour. It is
the free decision to trust in Christ's promises and to obey
Christ's commandments to repent and believe. On the other
hand, conversion is the act of God in making Himself real and
vivid to the sinner by warming his heart and giving him peace
and power.

It is in this second, and, of course, supremely important, process of conversion that the graces of Jesus are imparted to, and implanted in, the life of the convert. Conversion is generally proclaimed and experienced in evangelical Protestantism as a dramatic episode which can be experienced suddenly, so that the convert can specify the precise time and place when and where it happened. Nevertheless, this kind of experience is by no means either universal or necessary, because some of the indubitable saints of the Faith the validity of whose Christlike lives and convictions it would be impudent to question, can point to no such episode. They testify to a gradual apprehension of the claims of Jesus, and an equally gradual experience of the graces that follow discipleship. They would be concerned to record a number of significant episodes in their spiritual careers, and would insist that each of these episodes was characterized by a decision taken or an intention registered. What many of them would not say is that they associate a vivid experience of inflowing grace with any of these episodes. They have grown in grace, and that growth has been imperceptible at the time.

It seems to me that it would make for clarity in our Christian thinking if we reserved the word conversion for the dramatic experience, for there is nothing sacrosanct in the word itself, and those who cannot point to the day when and where their chains fell off and their heart was free should not feel that they are only the poor relations of their Christian brethren who can testify to a sudden experience. We should immediately be free to recognize conversion, in this more exact sense, as one way in which the grace of God comes to men, but not necessarily the only way. It depends on the sort of person you are whether this is the means of your salvation. It may not be the road for you.

How I wish I had known this when I was an adolescent. Instead, I felt that because I could not point to the day and place when and where I was saved, I was permanently in the dock having to advance evidence in mitigation of *my* criminal negligence of *my* Christian duty. Why could I not centre my Christian life upon a single act of surrender? Why could I not testify to an experience of peace and of certitude that accompanied such an act? Worst of all, it was impressed upon me that unless I did follow this path, and unless I could witness to such a dramatic transformation, my Christianity—such as it was—was of an inferior brand, if indeed I was entitled to call myself a Christian at all. It is clear to me now that there is more than one road into the Christian life, and historically the road that the majority of Christians have taken has not been the road of conversion (as I have presumed to define it), but the road of eucharistic worship.

Now, gentle reader, I am well aware that conversion and eucharistic worship are not entirely disparate, and I am anxious to avoid any suggestion that I am drawing a hard and fast distinction between two spiritual processes which at bottom are one. I believe they are, but I also believe that in emphasis, in the way in which we approach them, in the feelings that accompany them, they are distinguishable. Above all, I believe that the one is more individualistic and subjective, the other more corporate and objective. I will endeavour to draw out these distinctions a little later. It will be sufficient at the moment to assert that the apostolic primitive means of grace was in the celebration of the Holy Eucharist. This was both the converting and the confirming ordinance of the early Christian Church.

Without petulance, let me put it on record that until I made my own way to the discovery of eucharistic worship, I do not recall any of my spiritual mentors opening up that way for me. Eucharistic worship is the lost art of Nonconformity. The pattern of the Sunday services and the week-day devotional meetings in which I grew up was one of personal challenge through the medium of much singing of hymns, much saying of extempore prayers, and much preaching of sermons. The Sacrament of the Lord's Supper was an after-service; it was generally an afterthought. The emphasis, as far as I remember it, was continually on the individual response that I ought to make to the issues put to me, and the feelings I ought to experience as a result of that response. The Lord's Supper was an optional additional kind of service for those who felt like it, or who, because of their particular temperament, were likely to profit from such a celebration.

Yet the blazing fact is that the Christian Church was born and bred in another and very different atmosphere from this. The early Christians came together to sing and to pray and to be exhorted, but pre-eminently to celebrate the Eucharist. In this celebration there were two predominant and interwoven characteristics. The one was the eucharistic prayer itself—a great corporate simple act of thanksgiving for the mighty works of God in Christ Jesus, an act of rejoicing, of gratitude. The other was the obedient fulfilling of the command of Jesus to 'do' the acts of the Last Supper, with all their many associations of meaning and their symbols of the Christian truth and the Christian way, and to receive the effects promised to the participant.

This was the core of apostolic Churchmanship. What I am insisting here is that it was the core of evangelization as well. Eucharistic worship was the focus and the universal characteristic of Christianity. Whereas some might be dramatically converted, and others might grow in grace more slowly (such experiences were a matter of temperament and education), the general means of grace was attendance at the Lord's Table and participation in the great collective act of the Christian community. The centrality of the Mass in Roman Catholicism bears continuing testimony to this basic element in the Christian religion, but for me the Orthodox Churches, whose life I came to know at first hand when I was in Moscow, has ever since presented even more overwhelming evidence of this fundamental and universal Christian act. It would not be grossly inaccurate to say that Russian Orthodox Churchmanship is the Liturgy, and the Liturgy is eucharistic worship.

So long protracted and so often repeated is this Liturgy, this celebration of the Lord's Supper, that an Orthodox priest has little time left except for baptisms, weddings, and funerals. Coming, as I did, from a Church in London which has a large number of activities, to suit all tastes and meet what we reckon to be the various spiritual needs of those to whom we minister, I at first felt that the Russian Church was narrow and remiss. I wonder now whether the Orthodox concentration upon its Liturgy is not the choosing of 'the better part' while some of us are 'anxious about many things'. I shall never forget the rapt attention of the worshippers, the unmistakable sense of power, and, most of all, the pervasive feeling that something was happening to those who were gathered before the Lord's Table. At the risk of a somewhat crude over-simplification, I would put it that whereas many earnest evangelical Christians here would say 'Get saved', the equally evangelical Christians in Moscow would say 'Come to church'. In the two cases the hope would be that the supernatural grace of our Blessed Lord would enliven the sinner who is afflicted by his sin. The difference would be that, in the one case, the grace would be thought to flow into the sinner's life at the moment of his wilful act of surrender, that is his conversion, whereas in the other case, the same grace would be transmitted as the sinner participated in the corporate act of worship, obedience, and re-enactment of our Lord's Passion that is eucharistic worship.

I believe that the insistence on the former, as the norm of the Christian life, is factitious. By this very insistence the value and importance of the latter is obscured, if not obliterated. It is my conviction that eucharistic worship is objective, universal, and apostolic—the divinely ordained means whereby Jesus enters the life of the believer and begins that saving work which reaches its glory in the words of Paul: 'I live, yet no longer I, but Christ liveth in me.' Were this a book on the subject of Church unity I should wish to develop the argument that eucharistic worship is, moreover, the indispensable ground of reunion, and without it all our efforts to come to terms with Rome and Byzantium are but beating the air. However, I do not wish to divert attention from the simpler and less controversial subject of these pages.

How is it possible for the most ardent advocate of 'conversion preaching' to recognize the importance of this other great 'altar of grace'? I shall be content at this point if he will agree that the Table of the Lord has been neglected, that many would-be Christians have been deterred by the subjectivity of evangelical preaching, and that it would be an excellent thing if a recovery were made of the great apostolic practices out of which sprang a faith which turned the world upside down. Very well then, what is Eucharistic worship? What does it involve? How does the sinner set about it so that Christ's goodness is imparted to his soul? To those who desire a theological, historical, comprehensive exposition, let me recommend Gregory Dix's incomparable work, *The Shape of the Liturgy*, which has the unique merit of preparing the way for any other reading on this theme, as well as expounding it with erudite scholarship, and often with great beauty. All that I dare to attempt is a very pedestrian description of what eucharistic worship involves for the would-be worshipper.

TEN

Grace Available

TO the question: 'What must I do to be saved?', a question which receives quite simple and precise answers out of the mouth of the more familiar kind of evangelist, I will endeavour to give equally simple and precise answers. These answers fall into two divisions, or rather fall into two stages. The first is the participation required of the worshipper in the actual proceedings, the mechanism—so to say—of the service, the things he is required to do, with all the physical actions and the sensory impressions that such participation involves. The second is the participation of the worshipper in the spiritual significance of these proceedings, the attitude of heart and mind and will which the service implies and demands. It is most important to recognize that at both these levels of participation, the testimony of the Church is that grace is imparted—naturally more intensely and deeply at the deeper level, but not confined to that deeper level.

Let us imagine, then, that someone who is not a professing Christian, or who is but nominally attached to Christianity, has earnestly considered the character of Jesus. Let us further imagine that such a person has stood at the foot of the Cross and appreciated there those deeper insights into that sublime character, and now sincerely desires to be like Him. Finally let us imagine that such a person feels quite impotent in his own strength to achieve this strong desire, and is weary of being exhorted to do something, or to feel something, which— with the best will in the world—is out of his reach. It is the contention of this chapter that through eucharistic worship

These, these prepare us for the sight
Of holiness above:
The sons of ignorance and night
May dwell in the eternal Light,
Through the eternal Love!

This blessed work begins at the humblest and simplest level—the physical presence of the would-be Christian at this corporate act of worship. If we love God because He first loved us, then the 'initiative' is always with God. God is waiting for us. He is already there on the road we desire to tread. The sun of His love is already shining on our pathway. Without propounding any theory of irresistible grace, we can—I am sure—begin to think of our reception of Christ's goodness as a visitor to the seaside in high summer begins to think of the tan which will cover his skin. What he has to do is to expose himself to the sunshine, and the tan will look after itself. I realize that this analogy must not be pressed too far, but, in principle, grace begins to flow when we expose ourselves to the source of its radiating energy, just as our skins become tanned as we uncover them to the sun. That is part of what our fathers meant when they declared that there was no salvation outside the Church. The Church is the special, though not the only place, where spiritual events take place, and it is all-important to be there in order to profit from those events.

I find it difficult to understand the attitude of those who never attend a place of worship and then complain that they can see nothing in Christianity. What would they see in football if they never watched the game being played? Of course a man may sit in the most advantageous position to watch a League match, and yet may see little and hear little because he has been dozing throughout the whole proceedings. Nevertheless, even if he is more or less indifferent to and ignorant of the laws of football, something of its reality will assuredly communicate itself to him so long as his senses are not entirely neutralized by sleep. At the risk of labouring the obvious, I want to stress the continual importance of 'being there' in God's House and among the assembly of the Saints, for in a unique way this is the occasion of grace. If a man desires to be like Jesus, let him present himself at the time and place where countless multitudes of others like himself have found Jesus real and vital, and have felt the operation of His spirit upon their lives. There, as an equally elementary gesture, let him pay attention to the drama that unfolds in eucharistic worship. At its very simplest it is the setting forth of our Lord's Passion to reach the eye, the ear, the imagination, the heart, the mind, and the will, of those who are ready to attend to this supreme event. One of the most disastrous fallacies which lies at the heart of much Christian advocacy is that we expect a response *of* the whole man to the claims of Christ without presenting these claims *to* the whole man. For instance, how often has nonconformity presented its advocacy in intellectual terms entirely abstracted from aesthetic values, or proclaimed the beauty of holiness in the surroundings of ugliness, or housed great preaching in architectural squalor?

Again, when the senses have been recognized as having their place, certain of these senses have been selected as being fit channels of grace, and others condemned as being the gateway to superstition or as smacking of idolatry. Music—or, more often, just cheerful or glucose sound—plays a predominant role in Protestantism, as if God has a preference for the ear over the eye. If, however, a Free Church minister were to introduce the use of incense into his church services, in order that the nose as well as the ear might dispose people to worship and aid them in their search for God, it is likely that he would be regarded with something approaching horror by many of his devout members. Yet, if the nose is a less comely member, there is Pauline authority for giving it the higher honour! Much more important, however, is the fact, beyond any dispute, that the sense of smell is more nostalgic than all the others. I know that the scent of a particular brand of soap transports me, whenever I smell it, to a small hotel where, as a child on holiday, I was compelled to wash far more often than I thought necessary. A blend of colour, a musical line, the taste of a particular sweet, the feel of a particular cloth —what an important role each has played in my life. How effective is the power of each one to suggest a mood, or clothe a thought with meaning. Others may not be so susceptible to the power of smell as I find myself to be, but to me it is one of the most potent gateways to experience.

The point I am trying to make is that the senses are God-given gateways to reality, and 'reality is richer than thought', as Lao-tze says. This is for the Christian but an abstract way of saying that God imparts Himself to us through every aspect of His creation. Worship that centres upon the Eucharist is the enlistment of all the senses to proclaim Christ and to bring the worshipper into living contact with Him. There is something to see, something to touch, to hear, to smell, and to taste. There is action in the development of the drama of the sacramental recalling of Jesus' Passion; there is beauty in the spotless table, the gleaming vestments, the aesthetic pattern of the Liturgy; there is truth in the unbroken historical celebration of Holy Communion, quite apart from the truth of the tremendous assertions of the service as a whole; there are all the overtones of suggestion and imagination that this act of worship conjures up, and the myriad thoughts and ideas which are implicit in each phase of this 'Christ's life in little', as the Eucharist has been called. Let the would-be Christian pay attention to it, for here is Christianity presented as a living thing, or, rather, as life itself—the supernatural life which is hid with Christ in God. Men have testified in every age that 'there is life in a look at the crucified One'.

The third elementary stage naturally follows upon the other two. Let the would-be Christian be there; let him pay attention; let him take part. Obviously this third stage is an extension or a fuller expression of the second. Equally obviously, the degree to which he can honestly take a greater part than that of paying attention will depend upon his general attitude to Christianity—upon his faith or his lack of it. It would be very easy at this point to fall into solecism and to presume the very spiritual condition that eucharistic worship seeks to produce. However, without involving the would-be Christian in any hypocrisy, or prescribing for him the results that are yet to be reached, I want to argue that there is a part that the uncommitted attendant (to use the exact word) can play in the living drama of the Last Supper, and that it does in fact help to bring Christ to him and to bring him to Christ.

In general terms, what he can do is to realize that he is one of the 'dramatis personae' on the stage, and not a spectator sitting in the audience. This is absolutely vital. The spectator

G

attitude which, with the coming of television, is now recognized as an epidemic disease in modern society, is a mortal sickness when it invades the realm of religion. Going to hear a preacher rather than going to church, watching someone else going through the motions of worship rather than following the one who 'leads' it or 'responding' to the one who 'conducts' it—such are the all-too-familiar symptoms of this disease. Where the incidence of this affliction does not produce immediate spiritual paralysis it always leads to sterility. Nothing happens, because the spectator is inert and irresponsible. Nothing is required of him except criticism; and sooner or later he loses that faculty as well.

The Christian graces flow only in a dynamic environment. No one can say 'Lead me, Lord' until he is already in motion himself. It is impossible for a guide to lead a sedentary mountaineer. That mountaineer, however incompetent, must first strike out for himself on the gentle slopes of the foothills if he is later to be guided up the steep rocks of the mountain peaks. So it is with a Christian experience. That experience is to be found always on the stage, never in the stalls.

To forsake analogies, what does this mean in eucharistic worship? It means bodily participation in the unfolding drama. To stand or to sit, to kneel or to 'practise the Nonconformist crouch', are, of course, examples of this performance. They belong to the role of the actor in the play rather than to that of a spectator. The frequent gestures, crossings, genuflections, that are such a marked feature of worship at Western Mass or Eastern Liturgy, may appear extravagant and even superstitious, but they undoubtedly represent, at every stage of the Eucharist, this invaluable sense of participation. What is imperative is that our bodily actions should be undertaken as dramatic parts which even the least of us can and must take if we are to expect any spiritual blessings to follow. It seems to me that the danger of giving way to superstition by making the sign of the Cross at the mention of the Trinity, or by genuflecting before the Cross or the altar, is ludicrously small compared with the danger of remaining inert, deaf and blind and dumb in the presence of our Redeemer.

This bodily participation needs to be accompanied by the verbal responses contained in the actual Liturgy of the Eucharist. The repetition of such sentences as 'Lord have mercy upon us, Christ have mercy upon us', 'The Lord be with you, and with thy spirit' by priest and worshipper in the Mass and in the Liturgy (even the gabbled *Ave Marias* and the sing-song chanting of the Lord's Prayer and the Creed in Eastern Orthodoxy), take on an entirely new meaning when they are seen as means of grace within the framework of this dramatic act of worship. They are psychological devices whereby the mind and heart of the worshipper are disposed to receive spiritual gifts, and they are none the worse for that. The question whether such responses and repetitions are sincerely understood and uttered with conviction is irrelevant. When these responses and prayers have as their intention the inducing of a spiritual frame of mind they are acceptable to God, even if each word in them is not fully weighed, or each idea duly conceived. They may not be the house of prayer, but they can be the scaffolding within which that house is built.

To those who find these words preposterous, may I recommend the writings of any Roman Catholic master of prayer; and may I add the testimony of a Russian priest. He told me that the all-pervasive materialism in the midst of which he lived made it terribly hard for him to achieve an attitude of mind and spirit in which the things of God became real. Through the interpreter, he said to me: 'I sometimes say twenty "Our Fathers" in a row before the materialist barrier breaks down and the way is open for Jesus to come in.' Eucharistic worship provides the opportunity of response and repetition which clears the way and opens the door to the gracious power of God. The monotonous rhythm of chanting and the regular repetition of simple phrases produce conditions of suggestibility in which all sorts of mortal and temporal curtains are swept aside.

This, again, is dangerous and capable of being flagrantly abused, but I see no valid reason why the Church should eschew such opportunities if it believes that anything which helps a man to receive into his soul the grace of God is infinitely worth-while. Only when such God-given devices are prostituted to other uses are they suspect and damnable. No one could deny that these physical and articulate elements, when employed in other spheres and for other ends, have paved the way for the success of Fascism and the more disreputable sects. In unscrupulous or undisciplined hands, this sort of psychological bridge, which is called suggestibility, should be avoided like the plague. The Christian rite of Holy Communion, by its disciplined structure, and by its strict adherence to the basic tenets of Christianity from which no part of the service strays, provides a complete safeguard against all these abuses. It applies these means of spiritual communication to their proper function, and sets them within their God-intended framework.

Thus to the question, By what means are the graces of the Christian life communicated to the would-be Christian? the historical answer of the Church is that they are made available sacramentally through the medium of worship which is centred upon the Eucharist. I have endeavoured to describe some of the more elementary factors in this means of grace; what have been called 'the lower levels of prayer'. I am completely satisfied that one of the prime reasons for the apparent irrelevance of Christianity in the eyes of so many genuine seekers after truth today is the neglect of these humble means of access to spiritual reality. I am equally certain that Protestantism in general, and the Nonconformity in which I have been reared in particular, has lamentably neglected these factors in its Church life and worship. The Nemesis has been that the less intelligent and responsible sects have monopolized such factors, have let them loose, or have encouraged them in conditions of indiscipline and licence. No one can doubt the immense, if temporary, impact that recent large evangelical efforts have made on groups of people made suggestible by these simple media, of which I have been treating. Here is part of the power which, properly directed, is the power of God unto salvation.

For its fulfilment, however, there must be an intellectual

and spiritual participation in eucharistic worship to accompany
these more elementary ways of coming into touch with God
through Jesus Christ. In the concluding words of this short
book I must try to say something about them. Those who have
cherished the Sacrament of the Lord's Supper (in whatever
form the Church to which they belong has celebrated this
Sacrament) are at pains to say that no concise presentation of
its meaning can be made, because it is so much richer than
thought. They are equally anxious to insist that to equate this
sacramental worship with any one set of ideas or theological
dogmas is so totally inadequate as to be almost blasphemous.
There are within it all the essential elements of Christian
doctrine. It is a sacrament, a sacrifice, a communion, a
remembrance, a re-enactment, a dedication, an intercession.
Any Church which emphasizes one aspect of this central act
of Christian worship to the exclusion of others is schismatic.

Yet underlying the many ideas and principles which animate
it there is always the idea of sacrifice, that is, of offering;
sacrifice is the basic theme. That, after all, is only to be
expected, for there can be no reasonable doubt that the
dominant idea in the mind of any converted Jew, when he
thought of Jesus and His Cross, was an idea saturated with
the notion of sacrifice. Indeed, the words of Jesus Himself
about Himself and His Cross would be unintelligible except
in terms of sacrifice.

This concept of sacrifice was the great theme of the earliest
Christian writings and evangelism, and the keynote of Pauline
advocacy. This truth is nowhere better presented than in the
great Easter proclamation derived from Paul's letters and
enshrined in the earliest Liturgies of the Christian Church:

> *Christ our passover is sacrified for us: therefore let us keep the
> feast;*
> *Not with the old leaven, nor with the leaven of malice and
> wickedness: but with the unleavened bread of sincerity and
> truth.*
> *Christ being raised from the dead dieth no more: death hath no
> more dominion over Him.*

For that He died, He died unto sin once: but in that He liveth, He liveth unto God.

Likewise reckon ye also yourselves to be dead indeed unto sin: but alive unto God through Jesus Christ our Lord.

Christ is risen from the dead: and become the firstfruits of them that slept.

For since by man came death: by man came also the resurrection of the dead.

For as in Adam all die: even so in Christ shall all be made alive.

But thanks be to God: which giveth us the victory through our Lord Jesus Christ.

I have quoted this *in extenso* because it is through and through sacrificial. The operating and governing idea is the self-offering of Christ. We share in His victory as we are offered with and in Him. When, therefore, we think of eucharistic worship as being essentially sacrificial, we are not making an arbitrary selection from among many interpretations of its meaning; we are approaching the fundamental meaning upon which all the others are raised.

In making this point, which I believe to be valid, I am deliberately using the words 'sacrifice' and 'offering' in a general sense, and am not specifying any particular theories of sacrifice. I know that this is a vast and complicated subject, and I am no expert in it. However, neither were those who first celebrated the sacrifice of Calvary in the midst of the pagan empire of Rome. What they were sure about was that Christ had offered Himself for them, that His offering had transformed their world, and they could thereafter offer themselves to God. Moreover, they realized that it was because Jesus had made a *perfect* sacrifice that their *imperfect* sacrifice was now possible and acceptable. Every part of primitive eucharistic worship was shot through with the thought of sacrifice, and through that expression of sacrifice it became a means of grace—a way of coming to Jesus and of sharing His life. So I believe it is still.

ELEVEN

Four Acts of Offering

' JESUS comes with all His grace' as we make offering at His table, but the Sacrament of the Lord's Supper, even as it was celebrated in the earliest Christian days, was not an undifferentiated exercise of offering in the name of Jesus. There was a clearly defined structure and an equally clearly defined process of worship.

It is not arbitrary or artificial to think of four elements in that structure, and four stages in that process. I will presume some acquaintance on the reader's part with the Order of Holy Communion and the Roman Catholic Mass, and with the Eastern Liturgies. With the Anglican order especially in mind, I suggest that the four elements and stages are:

1. The Pre-Communion (Synaxis) which consists of the proclamation of the Christian Faith and the proclamation of its requirements; the offering of our assent to the Commandments, to the Word of God and to the Creed; and the spiritual and temporal obligations that rest upon the Christian.

2. The Offertory which, once upon a time, was the bringing of the very elements from which the bread and wine were selected, and which now is confined to the bringing of money, but which, in both cases, is the expression of our material and temporal commitment to Christianity.

3. The Eucharistic Prayer—the spiritual core of this act of worship, in which praise and thanks and adoration are offered to God for His great Salvation. We recollect and in the drama of the Last Supper, re-enact, the offering up of Jesus Christ to God as the sufficient Sacrifice for sin and as the perfect Saviour of the World.

4. The Communion, in which Jesus offers Himself to us under the symbols of the bread and wine. As we take

Him under those symbols, so we are offered with Him in
His body for the perfecting of the work of which He is
the first fruits.

In each of these acts of offering, and superlatively in the
completed unity of which they all play a part, the spiritual
effectiveness of this eucharistic worship is to be found.
Moreover this effectiveness is heightened by the clear perception of these distinguishable acts of sacrifice. Something
of the grace of our Lord Jesus Christ is, as I have said, imparted to those who can offer no more than the penitent
thief offered (and maybe he was not even penitent). He was
just there, and he saw Jesus dying. He was actually dying with
Jesus, and he spoke of a Kingdom of which he knew next to
nothing and believed in even less. Yet there was 'life in a
look' for him, and so there may be for us. Nevertheless, the
fullness of grace, which is the fullness of Christ, is for those who
make their offering of heart and mind and will at this great
spiritual Feast spread for all men. Let us consider, then, this
objective offering of what we have, and what we are, at each
of these distinguishable spiritual stages in the Holy Eucharist.

I

The Western Mass, the Eastern Liturgy, and the longer forms
of Protestant Holy Communion (I find little value in what
are called shorter forms of Holy Communion) all begin with a
presentation of the Christian Faith, a setting forth of its
standards and its requirements. We know that this was the
part of the service which was intended, not only for those who
were seeking salvation, but also (as a kind of manifesto of
Christianity) for all who cared to hear it. We know also that
in Western Christendom it came to be called the 'Mass of the
Catechumens', and corresponded to the confirmation class or
preparation class for Church Membership in the Church of
today. Until the catechumen, the would-be communicant,
was able to give his assent to the Pre-Communion, he was
required to leave when this part of the service was concluded.
Although, of course, more was required of him than an act of

assent to a number of assertions about God and his relationship to God through Jesus Christ, and about his obligations
under God because of what that relationship with Jesus Christ
did for him, those acts of assent constituted an absolute condition which had to be fulfilled. It was impossible for a man
to be a Christian and to partake of the blessings and privileges
of Christianity unless, and until, he had accepted its basic
beliefs. So it is still.

I resist most vigorously the idea that conversion comes
first and theology follows after. This is nonsensical, for
there is inevitably some basis of theology, however small, in
any evangelical appeal and its response. It is also imper-
missible, for the overt neglect of theology in that evangelical
appeal and response means that the theology which is nevertheless present is certain to be vague, slipshod, and unworthy.
There is no avoiding this issue of belief at the very earliest
stages of the Christian pilgrimage, and there are many on the
fringe of Christianity at the present time for whom this
question of belief sets up an impassable barrier (unless they
are prepared to 'climb up some other way'—and, all honour
to them, they are not).

It has been a serious barrier for me, and so it remains.
In one form it is impassable for me. If I am required to have
an inward sense of certitude about the tenets of Christianity
before I can enjoy the sense of sins forgiven and fellowship
in the goodness of Christ, then Christianity is still beyond my
reach. If the emphasis is subjective in this intellectual realm
—that is to say, if I must know myself to be free of doubt
before I can give my assent to Christian dogma—then like
multitudes of my contemporaries, I shall have to remain an
agnostic. What a release I found from that kind of prison
when I discovered another and more objective emphasis in
eucharistic worship which, although it does not clear up all
my doubts, yet clears the way for me to take those doubts
with me into the Christian life, and there, I pray, to deal with
them more effectively. What is required of me is not subjective certitude, but an act of trust. I am bidden to offer
myself upon the altar of the Christian claims. Here presented

H

to me in the first part of the Sacrament of the Lord's Supper is the Christian manifesto. Some of it I already believe; some of it I doubt; some of it I do not understand; all of it is beyond my unaided powers to comprehend fully. I think of Jesus; I look to His Cross, and I say: 'Master, I will adventure my mind upon You and Your words, and I will try to build my life on them as a house built on a rock. Master, You will not require of me now to accept every word that belongs to this sacramental service, for I cannot. Master, You will permit me to hold back my assent from certain of those words which here and now affront my honest thinking. Master, I accept as an act of trust these tremendous assertions and claims. May I come into Your Church, that my offering may be accepted and ratified.'

This is the offering up of the mind to God. Like all other human activities, the words in which we try to describe it are very imperfect. I must add a word about one problem that this offering up of the mind leaves unrecognized. I have no right to offer up my mind to God if I am satisfied on other evidence that no such Being exists. I cannot put my trust in the Jesus who is the 'Son of God' to be worshipped in the Sacrament of the Lord's Supper, if I am convinced intellectually that He was but one of the great religious leaders who have lived upon this earth. If, on the other hand, my intellectual situation is not one of positive intellectual denial of the Christian claim, but a much more negative agnosticism, so that Christian faith is not excluded by a contrary faith, then what I am challenged to do is wilfully to offer of my mind to the great adventure of the Christian interpretation of the world and the Christian programme for it. That offering, I am sure, can be made by countless people without doing any injustice to their intellectual integrity. In most cases the first steps towards Jesus must be steps taken deliberately; they must be wilful actions which result in experiences which can be reached in no other way.

What I am contending for is the conviction that this objective offering of assent to Christianity, as a corpus of teaching and doctrine, can be made by many who from every other intellectual standpoint would feel compelled to withold it. I am sure that it is the way in which Jesus presented His claims to His disciples, and that it is the way in which the primitive Church challenged Jew and Gentile with the Gospel. Above all, I am sure that this same setting of the challenge today is the only one that can make faith the dynamic thing that it must be, and that can release many an honest and would-be Christian from an intolerable dilemma. Let me therefore come to the Holy Table, and upon that altar of sacrifice let me offer my intellectual assent to the Gospel. It will be an imperfect sacrifice; it will be the pledging of a mind perplexed and in part unresolved; but it will not be an unworthy sacrifice. I shall be 'betting my mind on Christ' (as I saw it described somewhere), and in the living content of that adventurous offering He will offer me His truth, and that truth will make me free.

II

We turn now to the Offertory which, superficially at least, explains itself. What more natural in a Christian service than to take up a collection; what more appropriate than to take it up for the poor? However, let us make no mistake about it, those who are content to think of the Offertory in the Sacrament of the Lord's Supper in such terms have missed the deep significance of this essential act, and will miss the beneficent results that flow from the recognition of its deep meaning.

The apostolic Church did not make the mistake of over-spiritualizing the faith. To them Christianity was the way to God, but it was just as realistically the way to live in the Roman Empire. The Church was the community of the redeemed—the new Israel—with all the careful attention to material and everyday matters that had characterized the Israel of old. Although instead of the old dispensation of the Law these Christians were now living under grace, the sense of community had been heightened, and not lowered, by the transformation. They were bound together in a covenant relationship with God through the redeeming work of Jesus, and this imposed upon them mutual obligations of the most comprehensive sort. The community life which resulted from the Pentecostal experience is described in two places at the beginning of the Book of the Acts of the Apostles. No one can read the passages at the end of the second and the fourth chapters of Acts without the feeling that for these Christians this communism was a perfectly natural expression of their new-found experience. In particular, this possessing of all things in common was the direct application of the injunction of their Lord to love one another. In order to fulfil that commandment they felt the overwhelming obligation to offer up their worldly possessions and to have 'all things common' so that nothing should separate them from their brethren in this new and wonderful unity which Jesus had brought to them. Moreover, they were confident that in this personal sacrifice they were now doing more than obeying their Lord; they were realizing the God-intended pattern of their social life, and would find in this common pooling of their resources all things necessary for their welfare.

To me this is the social Gospel. I accept it, and deplore the failure of the early Church to sustain it for more than a short while. For me this bringing together of the spiritual love of God and the practical community of man is the great glory of the faith I hold, and the supreme message for the Christian world I seek. However, I must not dilate upon this theme, but I want to record the all-important fact that, although this primitive communism was soon abandoned in the Church's practice, it has never been forgotten in its worship. The Offertory in the Sacrament of the Lord's Supper is the eternal declaration of the social Gospel. Here we are constantly reminded that the 'personal' Gospel has not a desirable appendage which is called the 'social' Gospel. It is at one and the same time personal, spiritual, corporate, and economic.

Christianity is a sacrifice of the spirit and of the body. The terrible story of Ananias and Sapphira is ethically preposterous, as well as unintelligible, on any other grounds. I have the strong feeling that we Christians have made too much of 'stewardship' as the idea which conveys our practical obligations in relation to our worldly goods. It is so easy to attach too much discretionary power to the office of a steward. That was precisely Ananias's downfall. Stewardship is a weak and loose word, and its popularity lies in the clear recognition that 'Christian communism' is a hard and exacting programme, with alarming and revolutionary results. A steward has at least a modicum of personal control over the goods in his charge, whereas those who set up the first Christian communities called nothing their own to do with as they liked.

I am anxious to stress this difference, because it is vital to an understanding of the sacramental Offertory. Were this a treatise on the practice in modern times of this primitive Christian communism, then many problems would demand examination, and a great amount of detailed explanation would be involved. It is the overall attitude to the economic side of life with which we are concerned here, and it is this attitude which is given expression in this part of the Sacrament. When a first-century Christian brought a loaf of bread, or a flask of wine, and laid it upon the Holy Table, he was offering under these symbols his world of goods and possessions to God, and, through God, to the Christian Church. This offering was as sacred as the offering of his mind and will. This sacrifice was as acceptable to God as any other that he could make. There was, however, a further and equally important element in this offering. From the very gifts that were brought by the worshippers were selected the particular pieces of bread and jars of wine which were to be used as the sacred elements of the Holy Communion. As in the miracle of the feeding of the multitude, the gifts offered to God in the name of Jesus, and blessed by Him, became suitable and sufficient for the needs of all. The prayers in the Mass which accompany this offering bring out this truth with beauty and with clarity. Thus this Offertory was also a means of grace, the doing of something by the worshipper which became the channel along which blessings flowed from the Divine Object of that worship.

It is astonishing how exactly the miracle of the feeding of the five thousand has been validated in the world of 1956.

If mankind were prepared to bring its gifts and resources, which it may well feel to be inadequate, and were to offer them to God that He might bless them, there would be found to be more than enough to go round, even supposing that populations were to continue to rise at their present rate. This is still a miracle, because it involves a supernatural view of earthly things which would transform society. Denigrators of the Communist régime in Russia and China should ponder most carefully this almost sacred attitude to material things, for although these régimes fall far short of the Kingdom of God, they seem to be capable of eradicating certain social evils which have proved incurable in the so-called Christian West. Some of their moral achievements appear quite miraculous, and, paradoxically enough, are beginning to create faith again in the Christian Gospel. If you remember, it was Bernard Shaw who defined a miracle as that which creates faith.

Is this a diversion from the broad path of this chapter? Certainly not. We are inquiring into the methods whereby the goodness of Jesus can be appropriated and enjoyed by men and women like ourselves. Our answer is that eucharistic worship provides that means, and each part of that worship adds its own peculiar contribution. In the Offertory, we make the sacrifice of the temporal and material life in which we 'live and move and have our earthly being'. Marxists are showing us the amazing transformations of character that follow on the heels of new attitudes to private property and wealth, and new appraisals the satisfactions that possession and material power have offered. What they have stumbled upon, and have clothed with a spurious scientific ideology, we can find in all its fullness in the teaching and spirit of Our Lord.

Those who will offer the material world to God in the light of the Cross of Jesus will find not merely the secret of the good society, but also the Christian graces required to safeguard that society and to use rightly the material world which is received back from God transformed and made sacred. To put that same great truth in another form: those who say that a family life for all mankind (which I call socialism) will work only when human beings have become Christlike can here and now come to the celebration of that family life in the Sacrament of the Lord's Supper. Let them embrace it there, and, through the Offertory in particular, Jesus will begin to plant in them those very Christlike qualities, in the power of which that divine society may be set up on the earth.

III

I turn now to the part of the Sacramental service which centres upon the Eucharistic Prayer (the great act of Thanksgiving), and re-enacts in obedience to Jesus His breaking of the Bread and sharing of the Cup. Words are poor things at the best of times to express the deepest meanings of life—just to write these words is an excellent illustration of this truth. The more I ponder this pre-eminent act of the Sacrament, the less I feel able to express (in formal language) what it means to me. I find, moreover, that the less satisfactory treatises on the meaning of the Mass or the Liturgy are those which attempt precise explanations or hard and fast dogmas. What makes me most diffident of all is the real sense of unworthiness and of spiritual frailty which pours over me like a flood when I come to this most sacred act at the Holy Table. Yet I know the truth of it and can echo Charles Wesley's words:

> *Jesus, we thus obey*
> *Thy last and kindest word;*
> *Here, in Thine own appointed way,*
> *We come to meet Thee, Lord—*

and, coming to meet my Lord, I have prayed again and again with Wesley:

> *Come, Holy Ghost, Thine influence shed,*
> *And realize* (real make) *the sign.*

The sign has become real to me. I do 'realize' certain elements in this central office of the service, and will do my best to describe what I have realized. I do so the more readily as these elements find their expression, in varying ways, in the official doctrines of the Lord's Supper propounded by the Church. I ignore the merely commemorative doctrine as being quite unsatisfactory, and as having no warrant whatsoever from the Church of Pentecostal times.

I make this quite personal explanation because it is so desperately important that, in describing the sacrificial nature of this third part of the Sacramental service, the most scrupulous honesty should be maintained. Magic and superstition are the decadent forms of a religious faith where honesty has given way to expediency. This decay has taken place again and again in the history of the Church, and particularly in relation to eucharistic worship, so that many Protestant Christians tend to shy away from something which seems to them to be an occasion of superstition.

Keeping to the general theme of offering, it is reasonable to distinguish two aspects of offering in this part of eucharistic worship. First, we offer our thanks and our adoration to God in the eucharistic prayer, and in its marvellous peroration:

Therefore with angels and archangels and with all the company of heaven, we laud and magnify thy glorious Name; evermore praising thee, and saying, Holy, holy, holy, Lord God of hosts, heaven and earth are full of thy glory. Glory be to thee, O Lord most High.

I heard Dr D. T. Niles say many years ago that 'Thanksgiving is the core of worship and opens the door to the incoming Christ'. There is no act of worship that is so objective as thanksgiving. It purges the soul of introspection and cleanses the soul from selfish desire. I have found that it clears out the channels that join my life to God, and for that very reason it is a prime means whereby the goodness of Jesus can flow into me.

It is almost a platitude to remind the reader that 'Count your blessings, name them one by one, and it will surprise you what the Lord hath done' is an adventure which does in fact yield the kind of result that it promises. I look at the Cross and I am filled with 'wonder, love, and praise'. There is much that I do not understand about that Cross, but I see all God's gifts to me and to all His children summed up in the dying of Jesus, and that experience is very close to that which Wesley describes in the words:

My chains fell off, my heart was free.

Secondly, we offer Christ—'Christ our Passover is sacrificed for us'. The best human offering that we poor sinners can make is utterly unworthy. It is corrupted by our sin and tainted with all our imperfections. We plead His sacrifice and lift Him up in our prayers to God and pray that we may be acceptable to Him.

This is not a piece of logic, and I could not subscribe the exact words of Roman Catholic and Eastern theology, that Jesus comes down upon our altars in the consecrated bread and wine, and His Body is crucified afresh at every Mass or Liturgy, or, to vary the manner of stating this dogma, that the actual Crucifixion is formally repeated at each celebration of the Lord's Supper. But I know what they mean, or what they suggest to me, with increasing significance. It is that now, unlike that day at Calvary, I can take part in the offering which Jesus has made, for I can be a part of the Body broken and the Blood shed. The Cross is indeed set up in Kingsway Hall on Sunday morning, and a real sacrifice is enacted there if I offer myself with my fellow-Christians in the Body of Christ with Him as our Common Head. As is so often said with truth, Christ has no body but our body, no hands to be pierced but our hands, and no heart to break but our heart.

I find to my comfort that Charles Gore, in the *Religion of the Church* (a Manual of Membership), expresses magnificently and convincingly what I have said so haltingly, and I will quote his words. 'The Eucharist is the great Christian sacrifice. According to the doctrine of the Bible the only sacrifice acceptable to God is a spiritual sacrifice: that means the sacrifice of a person, and of words or things only as the expressions of a person. In the Holy Eucharist we come solemnly before God, as His people met for the commemoration of our redemption, to present to Him the sacrifice of our persons and our goods, our alms and our oblations, our prayers and our praises. And it is our own symbolic gifts of bread and wine that are consecrated to become the body and the blood of our Redeemer, the body that was broken and the blood that was shed for us. Thus, by the presence among us in His glorified manhood of "the Lamb of God who taketh away the sin of the world", all our imperfect and sin-stained sacrifices are brought into union with Christ's one full, perfect, and sufficient sacrifice, which was once offered for us, but is ever pleaded in the heavenly places. Thus in every Eucharist the one perfect sacrifice is pleaded amongst us afresh. And, when we have fed upon Him, we ourselves are joined to His sacrifice; and in Him we offer ourselves, our souls and bodies, to be all together a reasonable, holy, and lively sacrifice unto God who made us. This is indeed the end of our being.' To these words my heart and mind say *Amen*.

Once again, let me add that it is not necessary to have formulated in the mind a precise theory of sacrifice in order to make this offering with meaning, and to be blessed in the making of it. Let us make the offering, however poor and partial it may be, and God will receive it and increase our power to give it. Without this central act in the Sacrament, surely the Communion which follows is stripped of its meaning. No wonder that those who ignore in Holy Communion almost everything that comes before the actual receiving of the elements (albeit in penitence and faith) derive so little from their participation in this service and find it unrealistic and unnecessary. This offering up of Christ, and of ourselves in Christ, is the absolutely necessary condition upon which depends the reality of the act which follows it. Unless we are first crucified with Christ we cannot rise with Him. We must first offer ourselves with Him as His Body to be broken, so that thereafter He may revive us in His Resurrection Body. Holy Communion with Jesus Christ is strictly the fruit of His Sacrifice and ours.

IV

So, let us come to the final offering, which again is composed of two parts. First, in the eating of the bread and the drinking of the wine Jesus offers Himself to us, and then, having received the gift of His supernatural grace, we offer ourselves to God, no longer as sinners hoping for salvation, but as servants ready and equipped to do His Will.

If I do not feel it necessary to write so many words about this last stage of eucharistic worship, let my few words be a kind of testimony to those in my own Church who, despite their indifference to certain elements in the Sacrament of the Lord's Supper, have yet known the bliss of His self-giving as they have eaten the bread and taken the wine. Perhaps, to Nonconformists in particular, this is the least unfamiliar part of eucharistic worship. Certainly in my experience as a Protestant and a Nonconformist it is the one that is singled out as being of unique importance. In one sense, of course, it is, but I have been at pains to relate it to the whole act of worship, and I would stress again that it is the culmination of many offerings and the fruit of a spiritual process which includes the sacrifice of the mind and of the material world, and, above all, the sacrifice of our Lord Himself.

Through all these, grace is mediated. But in them the flow of grace is implicit; in the act of Communion that flow is explicit. The apostolic means of grace was in the blessing, the breaking, and the sharing of the bread, and in the blessing, the decanting, and the drinking of the wine at the Lord's Table in obedience to His command.

This is the feast spread for us in return for the meagre loaves and few small fishes offered to Him. Millions of men and women have proved this to be true. Some have ecstatically appropriated the grace at the moment when the wine has touched their lips, but most have found that all that has gone before in the sacramental service has led them away from themselves and has rendered them indifferent to any immediate sense of blessing. In Livingstone's quaint phrase, they have believed that the promise of Jesus is 'the word of a perfect gentleman', and have had no doubt that the grace would reveal itself in nobler lives and richer service.

They have wasted no time looking at themselves while they might look upon their Lord. Their assurance has been the increased depth of their Christian understanding and the increased ardour of their Christian witness, rather than an immediate sense of spiritual well-being. So it is with me.

In one way grace is like sleep—it comes to some as they think of its delights; more generally it comes to those who have forgotten about themselves and are lost in thoughts which take them out and away until they wake refreshed in the morning light. I do not take the bread and wine expecting that, as I rise from my knees, I shall either see a bright light that will dispel my doubts and fears, or feel a surge of goodness in my heart. I think of Jesus; I see Him in the bread and wine; I confide in His offer; and I ask that nothing in me may impede the flow of His goodness. I leave the rest to Him, and I can testify to the practical effect—a life that is preoccupied with His will, so that there is less and less room for evil and more and more desire for His service.

That is surely the road which Jesus said was narrow but led to eternal life—the full Christian life. Let a man make his offerings at the Holy Table, and I believe that he will be disposed thereby to believe in the reality of Christ's offer, and also, and best of all, that he will trust in His Lord to fulfil that offer in the common round and the daily task.

The other part of this final act is the new offering that the Christian can and must make to God now, because Jesus has come into his life, and 'supernatural grace is implanted in his soul'. Immediately after the partaking of the elements comes a prayer of commitment. This prayer recognizes a 'bounden duty and service' to employ ourselves for Christ's sake as members of His glorious Body; but it is also the prayer that the grace that we have received may be safeguarded by the dedication of our lives, which now we present to God as an approved and acceptable sacrifice.

At last we have something to offer beside our need and our intention. We have been made fit members of the Body of Christ, to perform those acts in our day that the Gospels record as having been performed by Jesus long ago. Such acts can make up a Gospel for the world in which we live, and Jesus will use this Body (the Church of which we are members) to complete the work He began in Galilee and Jerusalem and Calvary and on the Mount of Resurrection.

So the offering that is made as the very last act of eucharistic worship has the new element of vocation and confidence and assurance in it. The purpose of our goodness is fused with the achievement of it.

TWELVE

Do This

WE have looked in these pages upon the spiritual beauty and power of Jesus. We have come to the Cross in order that that beauty and power may be seen in its essence. We have then asked whether that goodness of Jesus can influence those who see and appreciate it, and, if so, how this can come about. We have thus been brought back to the Cross, but by another way—through eucharistic worship. The grace of our Lord Jesus Christ is vouchsafed to us in many ways, but, pre-eminently, as I think, when we come to the drama of the Last Supper and take our part in the sacrifice of the Eucharist.

This book has not been about either the problems of the modern world or the private troubles of people in it, but at the back of the mind of every serious man or woman is the dragging weight of fear and foreboding. How much we need better men and women to master the moral problems which now baffle and break us! What can be done to raise the level of human conduct and to improve the quality of human character? To this question many answers are being given, many experiments are being made in the scientific, the economic, and the psychological field. Among them all the Christian Church claims that it holds the 'open secret', and until these experiments are rooted in the Christian Faith they must fail.

This is a tremendous claim, and I would dare to make it along with my fellow-Christians, but not in terms of the present condition of Christian witness and evangelism. I believe that the Christian forces need integration just as the individual Churches need unity. I believe that Christian preaching needs a living focus and Christian evangelism a point to which men can be directed.

As a Methodist, let me end with a personal experience. I

stand on Tower Hill and argue and exhort in the name of Jesus. I ask my hearers to vest their thinking in the teaching of Jesus, to venture their lives in His service, and to seek His Kingdom in penitence and faith. Very often, I am sure that they catch something of the Christian vision through my very imperfect ministry there. What can I tell them to do about it? I can tell them to do what I have done about it myself. I have taken my fears and sins and half-visions to the Table of the Lord, and in the Sacrament of the Lord's Supper I have found that Jesus Christ has come alive. That is what I must say to them, for that is the way in which Jesus will come into their lives and make them new.

'Ye therefore that do truly and earnestly repent of your sins, and are in love and charity with your neighbours, and intend to lead a new life, following the commandments of God, and walking henceforth in His holy ways; Draw near with faith, and take this holy Sacrament to your comfort.'